Competition in the Pharmaceutical Industry

To Dick Rippe,
with many thanks.

Meir Statman.

Competition in the Pharmaceutical Industry

The Declining Profitability of Drug Innovation

Meir Statman

American Enterprise Institute for Public Policy Research
Washington and London

Meir Statman is assistant professor of business, school of finance, at the
University of Santa Clara.

Library of Congress Cataloging in Publication Data

Statman, Meir.
  Competition in the pharmaceutical industry.

  (AEI studies ; 374)
  1. Drug trade—United States.   2. Pharmaceutical
research—United States—Costs.   3. Drugs—Generic
substitution—Economic aspects—United States.
4. Competition—United States.   I. Title.   II. Series.
HD9666.5.S79   1983   338.4'36151'0973   83-3880
ISBN 0-8447-3514-0 (pbk.)

AEI Studies 374

Printed in the United States of America

Contents

LIST OF FIGURES

1
Introduction

The ethical pharmaceutical industry exemplifies the process of "creative destruction" described by Joseph Schumpeter.[1] By constantly introducing new products, the industry has displaced many old methods of treatment and revolutionized medical practice. The stream of new products resulted from a growing volume of investment in research and development. The industry achieved its present research-intensive form in the United States during World War II and in the years following the war.[2]

As Paul McNulty notes,[3] competition in the Schumpeterian sense is a dynamic process that acts as an ordering force, rather than a state of long-run static equilibrium. According to Schumpeter, entrepreneurs constantly look for opportunities to compete by improving their products and production processes and by introducing new products. The result is competition through creative destruction (replacement) of existing products and forms of organization.

The competition described by Schumpeter differs radically from the neoclassical concept of perfect competition in which every producer is a passive price taker who adapts to whatever technological, cost, and demand circumstances happen to prevail.[4] The Schumpeterian entrepreneur changes the prevailing determinants of the long-run equilibrium and causes shifts in the equilibrium position of his industry. He engages in active rather than passive competition.

Around the time of World War II, new opportunities were created for pharmaceutical entrepreneurship by several scientific breakthroughs, by the demand for drugs by the military during the war, and by the general demand for drugs during the postwar prosperity. The increased demand and the new technological opportunities meant that potential rates of return in excess of the "normal" rate of return existed for ethical drug innovations. These potential profits induced innovation, growth, and entry into the pharmaceutical industry.

The attempts of firms in the pharmaceutical industry to take advantage of these investment opportunities yielded high rates of return in the early post—World War II period. The resulting rapid growth of the industry, coupled with the impact of regulation in raising costs, lowered the rate of return on drug innovation by the 1970s to a normal level (see table 2).

Organization of the Study

Chapter 2 contains a description of the U.S. ethical pharmaceutical industry and its change over time. The forces that led to high returns in the early post–World War II period and to decreasing rates of return in the more recent period are examined briefly.

The changing return on drug innovation relative to the cost of capital corresponds to a competitive process of adjustment toward equilibrium. The problems of the definition and the measurement of the rate of return and the cost of capital are discussed in chapter 3. Special emphasis is placed on the need to measure the internal rate of return and on the serious bias introduced when the accounting rate of return is used instead.

Chapter 4 presents the estimation methodology and provides estimates of the average internal rate of return for drugs introduced by the ethical pharmaceutical industry during 1954–1978. A discounted cash flow model is used for the estimation. Estimates of cash flows are based upon detailed data on sales revenue over time of large samples of individual ethical drugs, and aggregate data on ethical pharmaceutical research and development (R & D) expenditures.

The methodology and the estimates of the cost of capital in the ethical pharmaceutical industry are presented in chapter 5. The cost of capital, which is identical to the risk-adjusted normal rate of return, is estimated as a market-weighted average of the components of the capital structure. The Capital Asset Pricing Model, which deals with risk explicitly, is used in the estimation of the cost of equity capital.

Chapter 6 presents the evidence on the competitive behavior of the pharmaceutical industry. Finally, chapter 7 describes the incentives for drug innovation. It assesses the impact of regulations on the attractiveness of investment in drug innovation. Also, it discusses the possible effects of the increasing generic-drug competition and the shortened effective patent period on drug innovation.

Notes

1. J. A. Schumpeter, *Capitalism, Socialism and Democracy*, 3rd ed. (New York: Harper Colophon Books, 1975), "The Process of Creative Destruction," pp. 81–86.

2. W. S. Measday, "The Pharmaceutical Industry," in *The Structure of American Industry*, ed. W. Adams (New York: Macmillan, 1977), pp. 250–84.

3. P. J. McNulty, "Economic Theory and the Meaning of Competition," *Quarterly Journal of Economics*, vol. 82 (November 1968).

4. A number of studies appeared recently attempting to extend and refine Schumpeter's framework into an evolutionary theory of the response of firms to changed market conditions through search and selection. An exposition and summary are provided in R. R. Nelson and S. G. Winter, "Firm and Industry Response to Changed Market Conditions: An Evolutionary Approach," *Economic Inquiry*, vol. 18, no. 2 (April 1980), pp. 179–202.

2
The U.S. Ethical Pharmaceutical Industry

The ethical pharmaceutical industry is part of the pharmaceutical preparations industry as defined in the Standard Industrial Classification Manual. Firms in the pharmaceutical preparations industry (SIC 2834) are defined as

> establishments primarily engaged in manufacturing, fabricating, or processing drugs in pharmaceutical preparations for human and veterinary use. The greater part of the products of these establishments are finished in the form intended for final consumption, such as ampoules, tablets, capsules, ointments, medicinal powders, solutions, and suspensions. Products of this industry consist of two important lines, namely: (1) pharmaceutical preparations promoted directly to the dental, medical, or veterinary professions; and (2) pharmaceutical preparations promoted primarily to the public.[1]

Ethical drugs are those that are sold by prescription. They are promoted to the medical profession rather than directly to the public. The firms whose main field of operation is ethical drugs are part of the ethical pharmaceutical industry.

Ethical drugs were sold in the United States by 826 firms during 1975. The vast majority of these firms are small. The top 30 accounted for approximately 85 percent of the total ethical-drugs market.[2] The difference between the large ethical-drug firms and the small ones is not simply a difference in scale. The ethical pharmaceutical industry may be divided into two segments. The small firms sell drugs mostly under generic names. They do not engage in significant R & D efforts aimed at developing new drugs. The large firms engage heavily in R & D efforts, and they market their drugs mostly under brand names.[3]

The Pharmaceutical Manufacturers Association (PMA) is a trade organization of ethical pharmaceutical firms. Its membership list contains more than 100 firms. These firms are generally the largest firms in the ethical pharmaceutical industry, and the ones that invest significant amounts in R & D.[4] The analysis of the ethical pharmaceutical industry presented in this study focuses on this segment of the industry.

The Development of the U.S.
Ethical Pharmaceutical Industry before World War II

The modern ethical pharmaceutical industry is characterized by heavy spending on research and development aimed at the innovation of drugs. In 1978 the U.S. ethical pharmaceutical industry invested $1.4 billion in R & D on drugs for human and veterinary use, representing 8.2 percent of its sales.[5] This ratio of R & D to sales is four times as high as the 2.0 percent average ratio for all U.S. firms.[6]

The pharmaceutical industry did not evolve to its modern form until World War II. The drug trade, however, is very old. The Ebers Papyrus lists 811 prescriptions used in Egypt in 550 B.C.[7] The Arabs introduced drug specialization throughout the Mediterranean area and established the first apothecary in A.D. 754. Although most of the drugs were of no value, some were useful. Apothecaries were also established in Europe, and by the eighteenth century some pharmacies, especially in Germany and France, included well-equipped laboratories where pharmacists attempted to produce ingredients of known identity and purity on a small scale.

Mass production of drugs began in the nineteenth century. In Germany J. B. Trommsdorf opened the first plant specializing in pharmaceutical preparations in 1813, and others followed.[8] In the second half of the nineteenth century additional machinery was used to increase the level of production.

In the United States the Revolutionary War made it difficult to import drugs and led the Continental Congress to set up a manufacturing laboratory under an apothecary-general.[9] A major problem faced by drug manufacturers in the United States and abroad was the production of standardized drugs. Such drugs were produced in the United States in the second half of the nineteenth century by firms such as Merck, Squibb, Upjohn, and Pfizer. The Upjohn Company, for example, was established in 1885 by a physician who invented a process for manufacturing pills of uniform dosage and purity which could be crumbled easily with the thumb and provide the medication within the patient's body.[10]

The discovery of salvarsan, a drug for the treatment of syphilis, in 1910 by Paul Ehrlich opened up the field of chemotherapy by providing support for Ehrlich's theory that particular chemicals would kill particular organisms which harm the patient's body, without harming the patient. Even though Ehrlich's discovery is considered the breakthrough that opened the way to modern research and development, there was little systematic research work on new drugs by drug manufacturers until the

4

1930s. The discovery of the therapeutic powers of sulfonamide in 1932 and the demand for drugs generated by World War II transformed the pharmaceutical industry from a drug-manufacturing industry to a drug-innovating and -manufacturing industry. Harold Clymer, of the SmithKline Corporation, describes the industry in the 1930s as a commodity business.

> R & D as such was nonexistent in most firms ... it was in 1939 that I joined SmithKline; you can judge the magnitude of their R & D at that time by the fact that I was told I would have to consider the position temporary since they had already hired two people within the previous year for their laboratory and were not sure that the business would warrant the continued expenditure.[11]

World War II generated much demand by the army for existing drugs and new drugs. Sulfa drugs, for example, which protected soldiers from infections, were produced in large quantities in bulk form by firms such as Lederle and Merck and were transformed into powders and tablets by firms such as Upjohn, which developed a process of sterilization and packaging for sulfa drugs.[12]

Even more important in the evolution of the pharmaceutical industry into its modern form was the stimulus that the war effort gave to the development of penicillin, the first of the antibiotics. Although the properties of penicillin were discovered by Alexander Fleming in 1928, the antibiotic was never produced in more than experimental quantities until the war. In 1942 Pfizer, which had knowledge in the field of fermentation, developed a deep-tank fermentation process that provided the large quantities of penicillin needed for the war.

Penicillin was followed by a number of improved antibiotics, and it stimulated research into other therapeutic fields. The new research opportunities led to growth in firms which had some expertise in areas related to drugs. In addition, the distinction between fine chemical companies such as Merck and Pfizer, which supplied drugs in bulk form, and drug companies such as Parke-Davis and Upjohn, disappeared after the war as drug firms started to produce drugs in bulk, and fine chemical firms started to produce drugs in dosage form. In 1946, when penicillin was released for civilian use, Pfizer, which produced more than 50 percent of the total output in bulk form, found that the drug companies that used to buy the drug from Pfizer were starting to produce it themselves. Pfizer responded by acquiring a sales force and marketing drugs in finished form, and later by buying J. B. Roerig, a drug firm with a sales force.[13]

Entrants into the modern pharmaceutical industry included firms such as Sandoz and Ciba, which began as dye producers, and Bristol Laboratories, which was an extension of Bristol-Myers, a proprietary drug firm. Firms with no previous expertise in drugs also entered the industry. Phillips, the electronics firm, entered the industry by acquiring Columbus.[14]

5

TABLE 1
NUMBER OF NEW DRUGS INTRODUCED
ANNUALLY INTO THE UNITED STATES, 1940–1979

Year	No. of New Drugs	Year	No. of New Drugs
1940	14	1960	50
1941	17	1961	45
1942	13	1962	24
1943	10	1963	16
1944	13	1964	17
1945	13	1965	25
1946	19	1966	13
1947	26	1967	25
1948	29	1968	12
1949	38	1969	9
1950	32	1970	16
1951	38	1971	14
1952	40	1972	10
1953	53	1973	17
1954	42	1974	18
1955	36	1975	15
1956	48	1976	15
1957	52	1977	18
1958	47	1978	24
1959	65	1979	15

NOTE: New drugs are defined as single chemical entities or synthesized drugs not previously available in the United States, and do not include salts and esters. Diagnostic agents and biologicals are excluded, as are duplicate single products introduced at different times (offered as a single ingredient, also made available by other manufacturers), combination products (unless they contain a new chemical entity not available by itself), and new uses for old drugs. SOURCE: Paul deHaen, Inc., "Compilation of New Drugs, 1940 through 1975," *Pharmacy Times*, vol. 42 (March 1976), p. 4, and Paul deHaen, Inc., *New Products Parade* (various issues), Paul deHaen, Inc., New York.

The Development of the U.S. Ethical Pharmaceutical Industry after World War II

Expansion of research and development efforts in the U.S. ethical pharmaceutical industry in the post–World War II period was rapid. It was accompanied by increasing rates of drug innovation, as presented in table 1.

Sixty-seven new drugs were introduced into the U.S. market during the first half of the 1940s. The drug innovation rate doubled during the second half of the 1940s. It increased to 125 during the late 1940s, then nearly doubled again to 205 in the first half of the 1950s. It increased further to 248 during the second half of the 1950s.

From 1951 to 1961 R & D expenditures increased 295 percent, from $83 million to $328 million in constant 1972 dollars. Drug sales increased 66 percent, from $2,593 million to $4,319 million.[15] By comparison, the gross national product, in real terms, increased by only 31 percent during the same period.

The rapid growth of the pharmaceutical industry during the 1940s and 1950s seems to indicate that the industry was in a state of disequilibrium at some point near the beginning of the period. In the late 1940s, firms first took advantage of the fact that R & D aimed at drug innovation could now be a productive investment. During this period, the industry grew as firms attempted to capitalize upon the new opportunities through increased R & D.

The profitability of drug innovation during the early period was indeed high (table 2). The after-tax internal return on drugs introduced in 1954 is estimated to be 20.9 percent, approximately two times the comparable cost of capital of 10.7 percent. The internal rate of return on drugs introduced in 1971, however, dropped to an estimated 11.8 percent, approximately equal to the comparable cost of capital of 12.0 percent. The industry had apparently reached a long-run competitive equilibrium in the 1970s. The 10.3 percent rate of return for 1978 was lower than the 12.7 percent cost of capital. This, however, does not necessarily imply that the industry is not attempting to maximize profits. The estimated returns include compensation for fixed factors of production, such as plant and equipment. So it is possible that the marginal return (excluding compensation for fixed factors) is higher.

The average annual domestic sales of a new drug introduced in 1958 were estimated to be $6.0 million in its peak year (table 6). The figure for drugs introduced in 1968 was $14.9 million, or 148 percent higher than the figure for 1958 introductions. Expected peak average annual domestic sales of a new drug introduced in 1978, however, were estimated to be $21.1 million, only 41 percent over the 1968 figure despite growth in the overall size of the drug market well in excess of 41 percent (measured in current dollars of each year).

The decreasing rate of growth of revenues expected from new drugs can be traced to the increasing saturation of the market. In the 1940s and 1950s each new drug competed with fewer drugs than in the later period simply because fewer drugs existed. As the stock of known and available drugs increased, a new drug had to present special qualities to compete against established drugs. In large part, the decline in the relative commercial success of the average new drug since the mid-1960s can be attributed to this.

While the growth in expected sales of new drugs was declining along with the number of new drugs introduced, total R & D expenditures for

TABLE 2
EXPECTED RETURN ON ETHICAL-DRUG INTRODUCTIONS
AND THE CORRESPONDING COST OF CAPITAL, 1954–1980

Year of U.S. Market Introduction	Accounting Rate of Return (%)[a] Drug firms (1)	All mfg. (2)	Expected Average Internal Rate of Return (%)[b] (3)	Cost of Capital (%)[c] (4)	Difference (percentage points) (3) − (4)
1954	14.8	12.4	20.9	10.7	10.2
1955	18.3	14.9	19.8	10.7	9.1
1956	21.9	13.9	21.2	10.8	10.4
1957	23.7	12.9	21.6	11.1	10.5
1958	21.9	9.8	21.7	11.1	10.6
1959	22.0	11.7	22.3	10.7	11.6
1960	20.4	10.6	21.8	11.0	10.8
1961	18.4	9.9	23.0	11.0	12.0
1962	17.9	10.9	22.5	11.2	11.3
1963	18.7	11.6	22.5	11.2	11.3
1964	19.8	12.7	22.6	11.6	11.0
1965	21.2	13.9	22.0	11.6	10.4
1966	21.0	14.2	20.6	11.6	9.0
1967	20.3	12.6	19.4	12.2	7.2
1968	20.0	13.3	17.6	12.2	5.4
1969	20.0	12.4	15.8	12.2	3.6
1970	18.8	10.1	14.2	12.0	2.2
1971	19.0	10.8	11.8	12.0	−0.2
1972	19.8	12.1	12.5	12.0	0.5
1973	21.4	14.8	11.9	12.1	−0.2
1974	21.0	15.4	11.3	12.3	−1.0
1975	20.4	12.6	11.5	12.3	−0.8
1976	20.4	15.0	11.4	12.4	−1.0
1977	18.8	15.0	10.4	12.7	−2.3
1978	21.5	15.9	10.3	12.7	−2.4
1979	22.5	18.4	n.a.	n.a.	n.a.
1980	22.0	16.6	n.a.	n.a.	n.a.

NOTE: n.a. = not available.

a. Percent return on beginning-of-year net worth of leading firms from Citibank, *Monthly Economic Letter*, April issues, 1954–1981.

b. See chapter 4.

c. See chapter 5, table 18. The cost of capital used is the cost in the year when the R & D program leading to the drugs began.

drugs increased substantially throughout the period. Research and development expenditures for human-use drugs increased 178 percent, from $161.5 million in 1958 to $449.5 million in 1968. By 1978 they had increased yet another 192 percent, to $1,311.8 million.[16] Research and development outlays per new chemical entity (NCE) increased by 83 percent from 1968 to 1978 (table 8), outpacing the 41 percent increase in expected peak-year sales.

The increasing rate of R & D expenditures did not yield an increasing rate of new-drug introductions throughout the period. Although 453 were introduced during the 1950s, only 236 new drugs were introduced during the 1960s (table 1). The ratio of R & D expenditures per drug increased throughout the period and reached a level of $69 million in 1978 (table 8). The breaking point in the trend in drug innovation was 1962. There is no evidence in the 1970s that the rate of drug innovation or the low real cost per innovation that prevailed during the early post–World War II period would be approached again. Two explanations are offered for the reversal in the trend of drug innovation that took place in 1962. One is that the decline is due to exhaustion of the stock of scientific knowledge required for drug innovation. The other is that the decline is due to increased regulation of drug innovation and drug research by the Food and Drug Administration (FDA), and the 1962 amendment to the Food, Drug, and Cosmetics Act in particular.[17]

We will return to the debate on the causes of the decline in innovation at the end of this study. Whatever the reason for the decline, it is obvious that the combined pressure of declining commercial success of new drugs, coupled with the increases in R & D investment needed for a new drug, brought about a decline in the rate of return on drugs.

Notes

1. Executive Office of the President/Bureau of the Budget, Standard Industrial Classification Manual, 1967, p. 103.

2. IMS America Ltd, *U.S. Pharmaceutical Market, Drug Stores and Hospitals* (Ambler, Pa.: IMS, 1975).

3. Only forty-five firms introduced at least one new chemical entity (NCE) drug during the five-year period 1972–1976. See Paul deHaen, Inc., *New Drug Analysis* (New York: Paul deHaen Inc., 1976).

4. PMA member firms account for 93–95 percent of the total domestic ethical-drugs market.

5. PMA, *Annual Survey Report Ethical Pharmaceutical Industry Operations 1978–1979* (Washington, D.C., 1980), table 1.

6. National Science Foundation, *National Pattern of R & D Resources*, NSF 78-313 (Washington, D.C., 1978), p. 14.

7. T. Mahoney, *The Merchants of Life* (New York: Harper & Brothers Publishers, 1959), p. 6.

8. G. Sonnedecker, "The Rise of Drug Manufacture in America," *Emory University Quarterly*, vol. 21 (Summer 1965), pp. 73–87.

9. Ibid.

10. L. Engel, *Medicine Men from Kalamazoo* (New York: McGraw-Hill, 1961), p. 25.

11. H. A. Clymer, "The Economic and Regulatory Climate: U.S. and Overseas Trends," in *Drug Development and Marketing*, ed. R. B. Helms (Washington, D.C.: American Enterprise Institute, 1975), p. 138.

12. Engel, *Medicine Men from Kalamazoo*, p. 94.

13. S. Mines, *Pfizer: An Informal History* (New York: Pfizer Inc., 1978), pp. 88–89.

14. Measday, "The Pharmaceutical Industry," p. 254.

15. Computed from PMA, *Annual Survey Report* (various years).

16. PMA, *Annual Survey Report* (various issues).

17. For a summary of the debate, see H. G. Grabowski, *Drug Regulation and Innovation* (Washington, D.C.: American Enterprise Institute, 1976).

3
Disequilibrium, Monopoly Power, and the Rate of Return

As is well known from economic theory, competitive forces lead to a long-run equilibrium in which a perfectly competitive firm or a firm in monopolistic competition earns a return equal to the normal rate of return. A monopoly firm, however, will achieve a long-run average rate of return in excess of the normal rate. Thus, the difference between the average rate of return and the normal or competitive rate of return can be used to detect the existence of monopoly power if the difference is stable over time, or the existence of disequilibrium in a competitive industry if the difference does not persist.

The usefulness of this concept for empirical purposes is impeded, however, by several problems that arise from the definition and the measurement of the industry rate of return and the normal rate of return.[1] The following discussion analyzes these problems, starting with the normal rate of return.

Identifying the Normal Rate of Return and the Cost of Capital

If we accept the proposition that an expected average rate of return in excess of the normal rate is an indication of monopoly power or disequilibrium, we must first find that rate which may be considered normal. The Hart bill (S. 1167) uses a rate of return in excess of 15 percent lasting more than five years to indicate a "rebuttable presumption that monopoly power is possessed."[2] No basis is given, however, for the use of the 15 percent figure as the normal rate of return. Moreover, in general there is no basis for the use of a uniform normal rate of return for all firms or industries since the normal rate of return must reflect the level of risk. It is widely recognized in economics and finance that a higher normal rate of return is required for higher-risk investments and that differences in risk will result in differences in the normal rate of return even under conditions of pure or perfect competition.[3]

The cost of capital of a firm is defined as the minimum rate of return that it must earn on its marginal investment so as not to decrease the value

11

of the firm. It is well known from the theory of finance that a profit-maximizing firm would undertake investments as long as the expected rate of return (internal rate of return) is at least equal to the cost of capital, where the cost of capital is adjusted to reflect the risk class of the investment.[4] It follows then that the cost of capital of an investment belonging to a particular risk class is equal to the normal rate of return.[5]

The advantage of shifting our discussion from the normal rate of return to the cost of capital is that the association between the cost of capital and risk has been developed in a rigorous form, and there are methods for the direct estimation of the cost of capital. A discussion of the estimation methodology of the cost of capital in the ethical pharmaceutical industry is presented in chapter 5.

If the cost of capital, or the normal rate of return, is known, we are still faced with a number of problems associated with the definition and measurement of a firm's average rate of return. Here it will be argued that the relevant rate of return that should be compared with the cost of capital is the internal rate of return. The rate of return figures that are generally available, however, are accounting rates of return. Thus, we now turn to a discussion of the various definitions of the rate of return, and to an explanation of why the accounting rates of return are biased measures of the internal rate of return.

The Internal Rate of Return

The internal rate of return on an investment is the rate r such that

$$0 = \sum_{t=0}^{n} \frac{CF_t}{(1 + r)^t}$$

where CF_t ($t = 0 \ldots n$) are cash flows (cash outlays carry a negative sign, and cash inflows, a positive sign) derived from the investment. The decision rule for a profit-maximizing firm is to accept all projects for which the internal rate of return, r, is not less than the cost of capital of the relevant risk class.[6] This capital budgeting rule applies equally to firms that possess monopoly power and firms that do not possess such power.

It should be noted that sales of a new product by the firm may be made, to some extent, at the expense of revenues from another product by the same firm. Sam Peltzman, for example, estimated that if NCEs with a potential market share of 10 percent are kept from the market, the average prescription price in a therapeutic category will increase about $1\frac{1}{3}$ percent more than it would otherwise.[7] Thus cash flow estimates of a new product should be adjusted for any "cannibalization" effects on other products before the internal rate of return is calculated.

The existence of monopoly power means that some projects will yield

FIGURE 1
Optimal Investment Outlays for a Firm
in an Internal Rate-of-Return
and Cost-of-Capital Framework

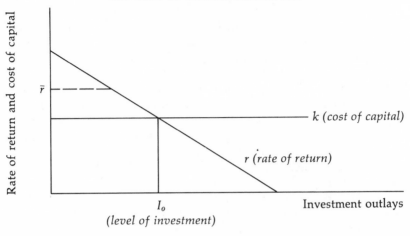

an internal rate of return that is higher than the cost of capital. Thus, the *average* internal rate of return of a firm with monopoly power in long-run equilibrium will exceed the cost of capital as illustrated in figure 1. The firm invests up to the point where the internal rate of return, r, is equal to the cost of capital, k. The average internal rate of return on these investment projects, $\bar{r}$, is higher than the cost of capital. The average internal rate of return will equal the cost of capital only if $r = k$ for every investment project, which is the case under perfect competition. In other words, the r curve facing a firm in perfect competition is equal to k at every point.

The figures for the average internal rate of return of a firm or industry are not readily available. Available rate-of-return figures are usually accounting rates of return. The validity of the use of accounting rates of return as estimates of the internal rate of return depends upon the relationship between them.

Accounting Rates of Return

There are two major types of accounting rates of return. One is the rate of return on equity, or net worth, and the other is the rate of return on assets. The rate of return on equity can be defined as Π/E, where Π is accounting profits and E is shareholders' equity. The rate of return on assets can be defined as $(\Pi + I)/A$, where I is interest payments, and A is total assets. All

13

measurements are made according to book values which appear in a firm's income statements and balance sheets. There are many minor variations of these basic measures of the accounting rate of return. The *Compustat* manual defines a total of twenty-five such variations.[8]

The computation of the accounting rates of return involves a number of practices which have been challenged.[9] One such practice involves the use of book values, or historical values, of assets and equity. If prices increase, then the historical value is lower than the replacement value of assets. In that case, the measure of the accounting rate of return using historical values will be higher than the rate of return where replacement values are used. Since the vintages of capital vary from firm to firm, and from industry to industry, the difference between the two measures cannot be expected to be constant, making it difficult to compare rates of return.

A second problem in the interpretation of the accounting rate of return relates to the practice of treating advertising and R & D expenditures as current costs rather than as capital expenditures. There is generally no disagreement that such expenditures are capital outlays since the fruits of these expenditures are not likely to be realized in the period during which they are made. Such expenditures are difficult to capitalize, however, because they do not represent tangible capital and there are no reliable methods for depreciating R & D and advertising capital.

Kenneth Clarkson adjusted rates of return, capitalizing and depreciating R & D and advertising expenditures. He found that the difference between the alternative definitions of the accounting rate of return can be substantial, especially in an industry like the pharmaceutical industry, which has a high proportion of R & D and advertising expenditures (see table 3). Clarkson's findings are supported by a number of other studies. "While each of these studies uses different methods for correcting rates of return and alternative data sources, the results they obtain are clear and strong—namely, that accounting rates of return in firms with intangible capital are biased upward."[10] Unhappily, however, the accounting rate of return, even when corrected for the problems discussed here, can be very different from the internal rate of return.

The Accounting Rate of Return versus the Internal Rate of Return

Ezra Solomon confirms the conclusion that variations in accounting practices have a powerful effect upon the measurement of the accounting rate of return. He adds, however, that accounting practices are not the only factors affecting the relationship between the accounting and the internal rates of return. Other factors are:

1. The economic duration of each investment outlay,
2. The time lag between outlays on the one hand and the

TABLE 3
AVERAGE ACCOUNTING RATES OF RETURN ON
NET WORTH, BY INDUSTRY, 1959–1973

Industry	Rate of Return Where R & D and Advertising Are Expensed	Rate of Return Where R & D and Advertising Are Capitalized
Pharmaceuticals	18.29	12.89[a]
Electrical machinery	13.33	10.10
Foods	11.81	10.64
Petroleum	11.23	10.77
Chemicals	10.59	9.14
Motor vehicles	10.46	9.22
Paper	10.49	10.12
Rubber products	10.11	8.69
Office machinery	10.48	9.90
Aerospace	9.23	7.38
Ferrous metals	7.55	7.28

a. It should be noted that sales promotion investments other than advertising were not capitalized for any industry for lack of data. In the case of pharmaceuticals, nonadvertising sales promotion spending is much larger relative to total earnings and to total equity than for any other industry.
SOURCE: K. Clarkson, *Intangible Capital and Rates of Return* (Washington, D.C.: American Enterprise Institute, 1977), table 16, p. 64.

commencement of net cash inflows on the other,
3. The time pattern of net cash inflows after they commence.[11]

Thomas Stauffer presents some evidence that the internal rate of return for pharmaceutical firms is generally lower than the accounting rate of return. (See table 4.)

Solomon discusses the difference between the accounting rate of return and the internal rate of return when the internal rate of return is constant over time. He uses as an example the case of a firm that invests $1,000 each year in a project that has an economic life of six years, and where the annual net cash flow derived from each project is $229.61 in each of the six years. The internal rate of return for such investments is the value of r, such that

$$0 = -1,000 + \sum_{t=1}^{6} \frac{229.61}{(1 + r)^t}$$

or $r = 0.10$.

The accounting rate of return for this firm is b, such that $b =$ (cash inflow − depreciation)/assets. In the case where the firm capitalizes all its

TABLE 4
ACCOUNTING AND INTERNAL RATES OF RETURN FOR
SIX ETHICAL PHARMACEUTICAL FIRMS

Firm	Period	Accounting Rate of Return (%)	Internal Rate of Return (%)	Discrepancy (percentage points)
A	1963–72	17.5	15.0	+2.5
B	1953–72	20.1	16.4	+3.7
C	1955–72	9.8	12.1	−2.3
D	1953–72	29.4	21.2	+8.2
E	1959–72	20.4	16.3	+4.1
F	1958–72	13.3	13.1	+0.2

SOURCE: T. R. Stauffer, "Profitability Measures in the Pharmaceutical Industry," in *Drug Development and Marketing*, ed. R. B. Helms (Washington, D.C.: American Enterprise Institute, 1975), p. 110.

investment outlays, uses a straight-line depreciation formula, and has reached a steady state with six projects in operation, we obtain $b = (229.61 \times 6 - 1,000)/3,000 = 0.126$.

The upward bias of the accounting rate of return compared with the internal rate of return, in this case, is consistent with Stauffer's empirical findings presented in table 4. Solomon also shows that where investment outlays change over time at a constant rate g, the gap between the accounting rate of return and the internal rate of return can be positive, negative, or zero, depending upon the rate of growth of investment outlays, as presented in figure 2. Solomon's analysis demonstrates that the accounting rate of return, even when corrected to capitalize intangible capital, is a biased estimator of the internal rate of return except for the special case where the rate of growth of investment outlays equals the internal rate of return.

Solomon limits his analysis of the difference between the accounting and internal rates of return to the case where the internal rate is constant over time. The removal of this condition upon the internal rate of return will lead to additional discrepancies between the internal and the accounting rate of return over time. Since the present study demonstrates that the internal rate in the ethical pharmaceutical industry did change over time, it should prove useful to extend the analysis to the case where the internal rate of return is not constant. The analysis is performed by extending Solomon's numerical example.

Let us assume that a company capitalizes all its investment outlays and uses a straight-line depreciation formula. It invests $1,000 per year, and each such investment generates a cash inflow of $166.67 per year for six

FIGURE 2

THE DIFFERENCE BETWEEN THE ACCOUNTING RATE OF RETURN
AND THE INTERNAL RATE OF RETURN
WHEN THE INTERNAL RATE OF RETURN IS CONSTANT OVER TIME

Accounting rate of return, b, and
internal rate of return, r (percent)

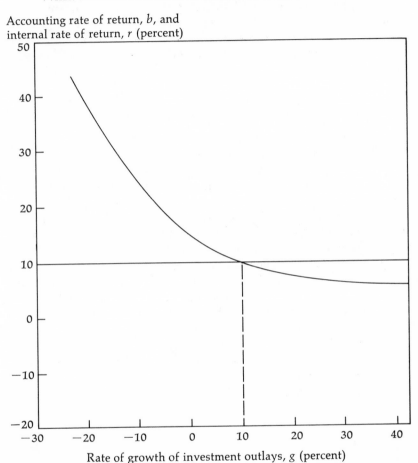

Rate of growth of investment outlays, g (percent)

SOURCE: E. Solomon, "Alternative Rate of Return Concepts and Their Implication for Utility Regulation," *The Bell Journal of Economics and Management Science*, vol. 1 (Spring 1970), p. 76.

years. The internal rate of return for these projects is r, such that

$$0 = -1{,}000 + \sum_{t=1}^{6} \frac{166.67}{(1 + r)^t}$$

Solving the equation, we find that $r = 0$.

The accounting rate of return for these projects is b, such that $b =$

17

$(166.67 \times 6 - 1,000)/3,000 = 0$. In this case, $b = r$, which is a special case consistent with Solomon's general conclusion that the internal and the accounting rates of return are identical when the rate of growth of investment outlays is equal to the internal rate of return.

Now, let us assume that because of changes in investment opportunities, investments made at the beginning of the year T and later, generate cash inflows of \$229.61 per year, while the investment pattern remains unchanged. The internal rate of return of projects started at year T is r', such that

$$0 = -1,000 + \sum_{t=1}^{6} \frac{229.61}{(1 + r')^t}$$

and solving the equation we find that $r' = 0.10$.

The cash inflow in year T is composed of five inflows of \$166.67 each, resulting from the "old" projects, and one inflow of \$229.61 resulting from the "new" project. The accounting rate of return for year T is b_T, where $b_T = (166.67 \times 5 + 229.61 - 1,000)/3,000 = 0.021$. The accounting rate of return for the other years can be computed in a similar fashion. The time pattern of the internal and the accounting rates of return is presented in figure 3.

The general conclusion that may be derived from the preceding example is that the accounting rate of return acts as a type of moving average. When the internal rate of return presents a trend over time, the accounting rate of return presents an "average" of that trend and previous trends in the internal rate of return. Substituting an average accounting rate

FIGURE 3

THE DIFFERENCE BETWEEN THE ACCOUNTING RATE OF RETURN (b)
AND THE INTERNAL RATE OF RETURN (r) WHEN THE
INTERNAL RATE OF RETURN CHANGES OVER TIME

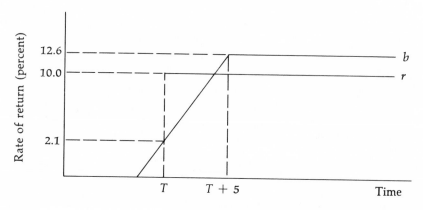

of return over some period for the internal rate of return, however, will not act to eliminate the bias. Using the preceding pattern of investment expenditures, for example, it can be demonstrated that if the internal rate of return fluctuates such that it is zero for three years and 30 percent for three years, the accounting rate of return will be stable over time at 21.2 percent, which is not an average of zero and 30 percent. Thus, the accounting rate of return acts to disguise or delay the presentation of trends in the internal rate of return. This problem may be particularly acute in industries in which the economic life of investment projects is long. In the pharmaceutical industry, for example, the life cycle of a drug may exceed thirty-five years, in addition to an R & D period that may exceed ten years.

The preceding comparison of the internal rate of return and the accounting rate of return makes it possible to evaluate critically existing assessments of monopoly power in the ethical pharmaceutical industry which utilize the accounting rate of return in the industry for their assessments. Henry Steele[12] and Leonard Schifrin[13] argued that the ethical pharmaceutical industry possessed monopoly power evidenced by "excessive profit margins,"[14] and a rate of return that was persistently higher than the average rate of return for all manufacturing corporations.

Indeed, observation of the average *accounting* rate of return on equity of the ethical pharmaceutical industry over the period 1954–1980 does reveal an average rate of 20.2 percent, with a standard deviation of 1.8 percent and no particular long-term trend (see table 2). Closer examination, however, reveals that the accounting rate of return of the pharmaceutical industry was declining relative to the average for all industries. The average return on equity for 1961–1970 was 19.6 percent for the drug industry and 11.3 for all industries. The ratio of the two averages is 1.7. Comparable figures for the 1971–1980 period were 20.7 and 14.7, with a ratio of only 1.4. It seems that the increasing rate of inflation in recent years served to inflate all return figures and disguised the decline in the accounting rate of return of the drug industry relative to the normal return.[15]

As noted by Simon Whitney, the relatively high accounting rate of return in earlier years in the ethical pharmaceutical industry may be explained by the relative risk involved in pharmaceutical operations.[16] A rate of return in excess of the average rate of return for all manufacturing industries does not indicate the existence of monopoly power, because the average rate of return for all manufacturing industries is not necessarily equal to the normal rate of return of the ethical pharmaceutical industry. The normal rate of return of the ethical pharmaceutical industry is affected by its risk.

Steele and Schifrin offered no evidence that the difference between the rate of return in the ethical pharmaceutical industry and the average rate of return for all manufacturing industries is not fully explained by a difference in risk.[17] In addition, the rate of return used by Schifrin is the accounting rate of return, which as we have seen, is a biased estimate of the internal rate of return. In the particular case of the ethical pharmaceutical industry, the preceding examples demonstrate that a declining internal rate of return can be consistent with a high accounting rate of return for a long period of time. Schifrin's argument that the high accounting rate of return in the ethical pharmaceutical industry is an indication of monopoly power is, therefore, not substantiated by the evidence he offered.

Notes

1. Y. Brozen, "Significance of Profit Data for Antitrust Policy," *Antitrust Bulletin*, vol. 14 (Spring 1969), pp. 119–40.

2. H. J. Goldschmid et al., ed., *Industrial Concentration: The New Learning* (Boston: Little, Brown and Co., 1974), p. 444.

3. R. Caves, *American Industry: Structure, Conduct, Performance*, 4th ed. (Englewood Cliffs, N.J.: Prentice-Hall, Inc., 1977), p. 69.

4. See, for example, E. Solomon and J. J. Pringle, *An Introduction to Financial Management* (Santa Monica, Calif.: Goodyear Publishing Co., Inc., 1977), chap. 13.

5. M. H. Miller and F. Modigliani use the terms "normal rate of return" and "cost of capital" interchangeably in "Some Estimates of the Cost of Capital to the Electric Utility Industry," *American Economic Review*, vol. 56 (June 1966), p. 343.

6. A comprehensive discussion of capital budgeting may be found in many finance textbooks, for example: Solomon and Pringle, *An Introduction to Financial Management.*

7. S. Peltzman, *Regulation of Pharmaceutical Innovation* (Washington, D.C.: American Enterprise Institute, 1975), p. 47.

8. Investors Management Services, Inc., *Compustat* (New York: Investors Management Services, Inc., 1975).

9. See L. W. Weiss, "The Concentration-Profits Relationship and Antitrust," in Goldschmid, *Industrial Concentration*, pp. 196–200.

10. K. W. Clarkson, *Intangible Capital and Rates of Return* (Washington, D.C.: American Enterprise Institute, 1977), p. 77.

11. E. Solomon, "Alternative Rate of Return Concepts and Their Implications for Utility Regulation," *The Bell Journal of Economics and Management Science*, vol. 1 (Spring 1970), p. 73.

12. H. Steele, "Monopoly and Competition in the Ethical Drugs Market," *Journal of Law and Economics*, vol. 5 (October 1962), pp. 131–63; H. Steele, "Patent Restrictions and Price Competition in the Ethical Drugs Industry," *Journal of Industrial Economics*, vol. 12 (July 1964), pp. 198–223.

13. L. G. Schifrin, "The Ethical Drug Industry: The Case for Compulsory Patent Licensing," *Antitrust Bulletin*, vol. 12 (Fall 1967), pp. 893–915.

14. Ibid., p. 912.

15. Computed from data published in Citibank, *Monthly Economic Letter* (various issues).

16. S. N. Whitney, "Economics of the Ethical Drug Industry: A Reply to Critics," *Antitrust Bulletin*, vol. 13 (Fall 1968), p. 803–49.

17. Discussion of the measurement of risk in the ethical pharmaceutical industry and its role in determining the cost of capital (or the normal rate of return) are presented in chapter 5.

4

The Internal Rate of Return of the U.S. Ethical Pharmaceutical Industry

The development of a drug and its subsequent marketing can be viewed as an investment project. As detailed in chapter 3, one way of evaluating such a project's performance is to calculate its internal rate of return, which is a measure of the return to each dollar invested. Technically, the internal rate of return on a project is the discount rate that sets the present value of the money spent by the firm equal to the present value of the money received by the firm.

A typical drug project begins with R & D and other capital expenditures that generate cash outflows. Following the introduction of the drug, sales occur over some period of time. Net cash inflow in each period is equal to sales revenue minus the relevant expenditures that are generated following a drug's introduction. To arrive at the internal rate of return on ethical drugs, estimates of all cash flows resulting from such drugs are required (see appendix E).

Estimating the internal rate of return is complicated by the lack of data on capital expenditures, other than R & D expenditures, that can be directly associated with particular projects. Data are available, however, on the average ratio of such capital to sales revenue. Consequently, this estimation problem can be solved by using the concept of the internal rental cost of capital (see appendix E).

Our method will be as follows. The cash inflow from drugs can be estimated from data for sales revenue of individual drugs. Data are also available for total R & D expenditures, and these are used in the estimation of cash outflows from drugs. Finally, the estimate of the internal rate of return presented in this chapter will be compared with the values found in previous estimates.

Cash Inflows from Ethical Drugs

To estimate the cash inflow from ethical drugs, we need to look at two factors. The first deals with the pattern over time of sales of ethical drugs. The second deals with the profit margin on sales, which is the proportion of sales revenue that remains after relevant expenses are subtracted. Once these questions are answered, the net cash inflow can be estimated by applying the profit margin to sales revenue.

New drugs that are the result of R & D efforts are either new chemical entity (NCE) drugs or combination drugs which are mixtures of NCE drugs. In addition there are drugs that are simply different dosage forms of existing drugs. All dosages will be considered here as one drug including the original dosage form.

The time pattern of drug sales varies considerably among drugs. Seven out of eleven NCE drugs introduced in 1966 by PMA member firms, for example, exhibited a generally increasing pattern of sales during the period 1967–1975, whereas the remaining four exhibited a generally decreasing pattern of sales during the same period. The 1975 domestic sales revenue of these eleven drugs ranged from $21,000 to more than $70 million.

The sales revenue of a drug over time may be described by a life cycle, starting with the market introduction of the drug and ending when its sales revenue drops to zero. The life cycle of the average drug introduced in a given year can be defined as the pattern over time of the average annual sales of drugs introduced that year. Assume, for example, that in a given year t, four drugs are introduced with the following life cycles:

Drug	t	$t+1$	$t+2$	$t+3$	$t+4$	$t+5$	$t+6$	$t+7$	...	$t+n$
				Annual Sales Revenue during the Year						
1	1	2	1	0	0	0	0	0		0
2	3	4	5	6	7	8	8	8		0
3	14	20	22	31	36	45	52	60		0
4	6	10	8	7	5	3	0	0		0
Total revenue	24	36	36	44	48	56	60	68		0
Revenue per average drug	6	9	9	11	12	14	15	17		0

The two significant characteristics of the revenue per average drug are that drugs are weighted according to their sales revenue and that the length of the life cycle is equal to the maximum life of any drug in the group.[1]

One conclusion that emerges from the analysis of actual sales data is that the average NCE drug starts its life cycle (see figure 4) with a period of growth in sales revenue (introduction stage), then changes to a period of relative stability in sales revenue (plateau stage). Although it is fair to assume that the sales of even the most successful drugs must eventually

FIGURE 4
THE LIFE CYCLE OF AN AVERAGE NCE DRUG

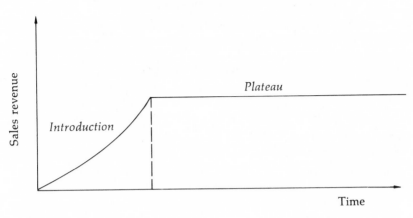

decline, sales of the average NCE drugs introduced in the 1940s still showed significant increases (in nominal terms) during the period 1967–1975. Sales of Premarin, for example, a drug by Ayerst introduced in 1942, increased from $28 million in 1967 to $59 million in 1975. Similarly, sales of Demerol, a drug by Winthrop introduced in 1944, increased from $8 million in 1967 to almost $10 million in 1975.

Although the length of the introduction stage varies, analysis of the data suggested that the average length of the introduction stage is approximately nine years. The annual rate of growth of sales revenue of the average NCE drug during the introduction stage was estimated to be 11.5 percent. The annual change in sales during the plateau stage was estimated to be zero.[2]

As noted earlier, combination drugs are mixtures of NCE drugs and may be considered as byproducts of NCE drug development. Although the R & D effort necessary for a new combination drug is on average considerably less than the effort required for an NCE drug, combination drugs generate considerable sales revenue. As table 5 shows, combination drugs accounted for almost 34 percent of total sales revenue of the 100 leading drugs in 1974.

Data on sales revenue of combination drugs were collected for a shorter period than data for NCE drugs. In addition, only samples of such drugs were used rather than the entire population, as was the case for NCE drugs. The narrow scope of the data on combination drugs does not allow for a detailed analysis of their life cycle, but there is no suggestion in the available data that the life cycle of combination drugs differs from that of

TABLE 5
DISTRIBUTION OF SALES REVENUE OF THE
LEADING 100 DRUGS, 1974

Drug Class	Sales Revenue ($000)	Sales Revenue (%)	No. of Drugs
Single chemical-entity drugs	1,161,502	60.6	61
Combination drugs	645,432	33.7	34
Generic drugs and medical instruments	109,749	5.7	5
Total	1,916,683	100.0	100

SOURCE: IMS America, Ltd., *National Prescription Audit* (Ambler, Pa., December 1974).

NCE drugs.[3] Thus, it was assumed that the life cycle pattern of NCE drugs applies to combination drugs too.

Since combination drugs are byproducts of NCE drugs, it is possible to define a drug "unit" that includes one NCE drug and a proportion of combination drugs introduced in a given year.[4] Table 6 presents the expected domestic sales revenue of an average drug unit that was introduced during the years 1954–1978.

Total sales revenue of drugs includes foreign sales in addition to domestic sales. To arrive at estimated global sales, the domestic sales revenue presented in table 6 must be multiplied by a factor representing the ratio of global sales to domestic sales. This estimated ratio is presented in table 7.

To estimate the net cash flows from ethical drug sales revenue, we need estimates of sales revenue, the profit margin, and the ratio of capital to sales revenue, as they appear in note 2. The previous section provided estimates of sales revenue, and we now turn to estimates of the profit margin and the ratio of capital to sales revenue. Arthur D. Little, Inc., estimates that the ratio of capital to sales revenue in pharmaceuticals is 0.60.[5] The estimation of the profit margin requires some analysis.

The after-tax profit margin can be expressed as: $M = [(1 - \text{Tax rate})(\text{Sales revenue} + \text{Other income} - \text{Operating expenditures}) + \text{Dep}_A + \text{Interest expenditures} - \text{Dep}_E]/ \text{Sales revenue}$. Depreciation as it is calculated for the financial statements of a firm, Dep_A, and interest expenditures are included in operating expenditures, and thus affect the tax payments of a firm. These two items, however, are not cash flows that are relevant as expenditures for the calculation of the internal rate of return, other than through their tax effect. Thus, depreciation and interest expenses are added back to the after-tax cash flow.[6] We also assume that wear and

TABLE 6

EXPECTED ANNUAL DOMESTIC SALES REVENUE
OF AN AVERAGE DRUG UNIT AT THE
END OF THE INTRODUCTION STAGE, 1954–1978
(thousands of dollars)

Year of Market Introduction	Expected Sales Revenue at the End of the Introduction Stage
1954	3,256
1955	3,222
1956	4,344
1957	4,996
1958	6,003
1959	7,233
1960	7,465
1961	10,897
1962	11,452
1963	12,867
1964	16,066
1965	17,467
1966	16,740
1967	16,537
1968	14,906
1969	12,800
1970	12,102
1971	9,842
1972	12,741
1973	14,187
1974	15,485
1975	18,051
1976	20,441
1977	19,718
1978	21,061

NOTE: The figures are five-year moving averages except for the 1977 and 1978 figures.
SOURCE: Appendix A.

tear of the capital stock requires expenditures equal to economic depreciation, Dep_E, to restore the capital stock to its original value.[7] If we assume that the accounting measure of depreciation is equal to the economic measure of depreciation,[8] then the definition of the profit margin can be simplified to: $M = [(1 - \text{Tax rate})(\text{Sales revenue} + \text{Other income} - \text{Operating expenditures}) + \text{Interest expenditures}]/\text{Sales revenue}$.

Arthur D. Little, Inc., estimates that the average tax rate on net income

TABLE 7
The Ratio of Global to Domestic Sales of Ethical Drugs by PMA Members, 1954–1977

Year	Smoothed Ratio	Actual Ratio
1954	1.17	1.20
1955	1.20	1.13
1956	1.22	1.13
1957	1.24	1.26
1958	1.26	1.33
1959	1.28	1.35
1960	1.31	1.36
1961	1.33	1.37
1962	1.35	1.33
1963	1.37	1.36
1964	1.39	1.37
1965	1.42	1.38
1966	1.44	1.41
1967	1.46	1.46
1968	1.48	1.44
1969	1.50	1.46
1970	1.52	1.49
1971	1.55	1.50
1972	1.57	1.56
1973	1.59	1.59
1974	1.61	1.66
1975	1.63	1.67
1976	1.66	1.67
1977	1.68	1.69

NOTE: A least-squares estimate was used with data on the actual ratios during 1954–1977. The ratio of global sales to domestic sales increased over time. The smoothed ratio was estimated as

$$RATIO = -0.015 + 0.022\ YEAR \qquad R^2 = 0.93$$

where $RATIO$ is the ratio of global to domestic sales, and $YEAR$ is the last two digits of the year.
SOURCE: PMA, *Annual Survey Report*, table 1 (various issues).

for pharmaceutical operations is 40 percent. It also estimates that operating expenditures, other than R & D, account for 68 percent of pharmaceutical sales revenue.[9] Income, such as royalty payments, derived from pharmaceutical operations other than through the sale of drugs was estimated at 2.6 percent of sales revenue, and interest expenditures were estimated at 0.6 percent of sales revenue.[10] Using sales revenue as a numeraire, we can rewrite the profit margin as follows:[11] $M = (1 - 0.40)(1 + 0.026 - 0.68) + 0.006 = 0.2136.$

We now have sales revenue data and the parameters that are needed to convert sales revenue into net cash flows. To complete the data required for the computation of the internal rate of return, we need estimates of R & D expenditures that are associated with ethical drug projects.

R & D Cash Outflows for Ethical Drugs

Estimates of the R & D expenditures that are associated with the innovation of drugs, and the distribution of these expenditures over the R & D period, together with estimates of cash inflows from drugs that were presented previously, will be used to estimate the internal rate of return on drugs.

Table 8 presents the R & D expenditures of member firms of the Pharmaceutical Manufacturers Association (PMA) and five-year moving averages of the number of NCE drugs introduced by members of the PMA. As was noted earlier, a drug unit is defined to include one NCE drug and a proportion of combination drugs introduced during a given year. Thus, the number of drug units is equal to the number of NCE drugs. Dividing the annual R & D expenditures by the number of NCE drugs yields an estimate of the average R & D cost of one drug unit, which is presented in table 8.

The development period of drugs, like the R & D costs of drugs, has changed considerably during the period 1951–1978. The estimated average development period of NCE drugs for each of those years is presented in table 9. These figures show a marked upward trend in average development time. The research period, however, was estimated to be about one year during the entire period.[12]

The estimated distribution of R & D expenditures during the R & D period is presented in figure 5. Of the total R & D expenditures for a drug unit, 42.5 percent are research expenditures, which are incurred during the first year of the R & D project. The remaining 57.5 percent of R & D expenditures are development expenditures, and these are distributed in decreasing amounts over the development period.[13]

The estimates of the total R & D expenditures per drug unit and the distribution of these expenditures over time can be used to estimate the R & D cash outflows that are associated with a drug unit. The development of a drug unit introduced in 1956, for example, took place during 1953–1955 since the length of the development period of such drugs was estimated to be three years. The research relating to such a drug was estimated to occur one year before the beginning of the development period, or in 1952. Table 10 presents the distribution of R & D expenditures during the R & D period of a drug unit introduced in 1956. Since all the cash flows that are associated with drug projects have been estimated, we can turn to the estimation of the internal rate of return on drugs.

TABLE 8
Global R & D Expenditures, Number of Drugs Introduced Annually in the Domestic Market, and R & D Expenditures per Drug Unit, for PMA Member Firms, 1951–1978

Year	No. of NCE Drugs Introduced (1)	No. of Combination Drugs Introduced (2)	R & D Expenditures for Human-Use Drugs ($ millions) (3)	Moving Average No. of NCE Drugs Introduced by PMA Members[a] (4)	R & D Expenditures per Drug Unit[b] ($ millions) (3) ÷ (4)
1951	34	n.a.	47.5	30.0	1.583
1952	30	n.a.	59.9	33.8	1.772
1953	45	n.a.	63.7	33.8	1.885
1954	34	188	74.1	34.8	2.129
1955	26	178	86.5	37.0	2.338
1956	39	184	99.5	35.4	2.811
1957	41	167	120.7	40.8	2.958
1958	37	159	161.5	44.2	3.654
1959	61	148	187.2	44.0	4.255
1960	43	150	206.0	41.0	5.024
1961	38	109	227.2	37.0	6.141
1962	26	108	238.0	27.8	8.561
1963	17	107	267.1	23.8	11.223
1964	15	94	278.3	18.4	15.125
1965	23	67	328.6	17.8	18.461
1966	11	43	374.4	16.6	22.554
1967	23	30	412.4	15.2	27.132
1968	11	47	449.5	13.8	32.572
1969	8	24	505.8	14.4	35.125
1970	16	34	565.8	11.8	47.949
1971	14	23	628.8	13.0	48.369
1972	10	14	666.8	14.6	45.671
1973	17	13	752.5	14.4	52.257
1974	16	14	858.5	14.4	59.618
1975	15	26	973.5	16.4	59.360
1976	14	12	1,067.8	16.8	63.560
1977	20	22	1,181.8	17.7	66.768
1978	19	11	1,311.2	19.0	69.011

NOTE: Ethical-drug sales of PMA members constitute 93–95 percent of the total domestic ethical drug market. Accordingly, only drugs introduced by PMA members were counted. NCE drugs include diagnostic agents and biologicals. Data on R & D expenditures for human-use drugs were available only for the period starting in 1961. Data on R & D expenditures before 1961 include R & D for veterinary-use drugs. The proportion of R & D for human-use drugs out of the total of R & D for human-use and veterinary drugs was esti-

TABLE 9

AVERAGE DEVELOPMENT PERIOD FOR NCE DRUGS
INTRODUCED EACH YEAR DURING 1951–1978

Year of U.S. Market Introduction	Average Development Time (years)
1951	1
1952	2
1953	2
1954	2
1955	3
1956	3
1957	3
1958	4
1959	4
1960	4
1961	5
1962	5
1963	6
1964	6
1965	6
1966	7
1967	7
1968	7
1969	8
1970	8
1971	8
1972	9
1973	9
1974	9
1975	10
1976	10
1977	10
1978	11

SOURCE: Appendix B.

mated as 95 percent of total R & D expenditures, based upon the average proportion during 1961–1965. Research-and-development figures include expenditures by the firms in the United States and abroad.

a. A five-year moving average was used to reduce the variation in the annual rate of drug introduction. The figures for 1951 and 1977 are three-year moving averages. The 1978 figure is not an average.

b. As is explained in the text, the number of drug units is identical to the number of NCE drugs.

SOURCE: Data on R & D expenditures for human-use drugs are available for members of the PMA only. Lists of drugs were obtained from Paul deHaen, Inc., *New Product Survey* (New York, various years). Data for R & D expenditures are from Pharmaceutical Manufacturers Association, *Annual Survey Report, Ethical Pharmaceutical Industry Operations* (Washington, D.C., various issues). Annual membership lists of PMA members were obtained from the PMA.

FIGURE 5
The Distribution of R & D Expenditures for a Drug Unit

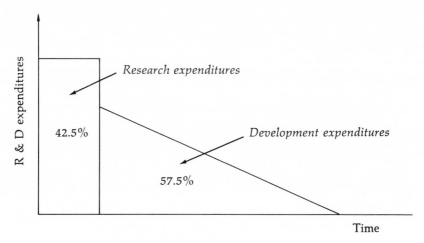

The Internal Rate of Return on Ethical Drugs

The estimates of the average internal rate of return on ethical drugs are presented in table 2. Two issues had to be dealt with in constructing these estimates. First, available data on ethical drug sales revenue indicate that the life cycle of the average drug is at least thirty-five years. Although it was not possible to estimate the length of the life cycle of ethical drugs, additional

TABLE 10
Distribution of R & D Expenditures for One Drug Unit Introduced in 1956

Year	Fraction of R & D Expenditures (1)	Total R & D Expenditures per Drug Unit ($ millions) (2)	R & D Expenditures for a 1956 Drug Unit ($ millions) (1) × (2)
1952	0.425	1.772	0.753
1953	0.319	1.885	0.601
1954	0.192	2.129	0.409
1955	0.064	2.338	0.149
	1.000		

SOURCE: Total R & D expenditures per drug unit are from table 8. Decimals are from figure 5.

30

life cycle years beyond thirty-five did not affect the estimated rate of return significantly. Computing the estimated rate of return under the assumption of a fifty-year life cycle, for example, added no more than 0.2 percentage points to the estimate of the rate of return.

A second estimation problem concerns the ratio of global sales revenue to domestic sales revenue of the U.S. ethical pharmaceutical industry. This ratio has been generally increasing since the early 1950s, implying that growth in foreign sales was faster than growth in the domestic market. Analysis of foreign markets, however, indicates that exports are not likely to continue to grow at a faster rate than the domestic market in the future.[14] The rate of return was estimated under the assumption that the ratio of global to domestic sales stabilizes at the projected 1980 level of 1.74. An alternative assumption, that this ratio will stabilize at the projected 1990 level of 1.96, yielded an increase of no more than 0.4 percentage points in the estimated rate of return.

Estimates of accounting rates of return of the pharmaceutical industry and their bias as measures of the internal rate of return are discussed in chapter 3. There are also estimates of the internal rate of return in the pharmaceutical industry that use the discounted-cash-flow model. Martin Baily, for example, arrived at an estimate by formulating an R & D function (cash outflows) and a returns function (cash inflows).[15]

Baily used regression analysis on company data to estimate his equations. Combining them in a discounted-cash-flow model, he estimated that the pretax internal rate of return in the pharmaceutical industry was 35 percent in 1954 and declined to 25 percent in 1961. Although Baily did not estimate the rate of return for the post-1961 period, he indicated that it is likely that the rate of return declined further during those years.

Applying a 40 percent average tax level to Baily's figure for 1954 yields an after-tax rate of return of 21 percent, which is nearly identical to the 20.9 percent reported in the present study.[16] Baily's 15 percent after-tax figure for 1961, however, does differ substantially from the 23.0 percent rate of return reported for that year in the present study.

Baily's estimate suffers from a number of difficulties. Henry Grabowski estimated Baily's R & D function using five additional years of data and found that the coefficient of Baily's measure of depletion of research opportunities, one of the two independent variables in Baily's function, becomes statistically insignificant.[17] In addition, Baily assumed that the time lag between R & D expenditures and the introduction of drugs is constant, whereas evidence in the present study points to an increasing lag pattern.

Baily also assumed that the length of the life cycle of drugs is seventeen years, which is the length of the patent period. Evidence presented in this study, however, indicates a life cycle that is more than double Baily's estimate. In addition, Baily's drug life cycle pattern, arrived at through regres-

TABLE 11
AVERAGE INTERNAL RATE OF RETURN FOR SIX
PHARMACEUTICAL FIRMS

Firm	Period	Internal Rate of Return (percent)
A	1963–72	15.0
B	1953–72	16.4
C	1955–72	12.1
D	1959–72	21.2
E	1959–72	16.3
F	1958–72	13.1

SOURCE: Stauffer, "Profitability Measures in the Pharmaceutical Industry," table 3.

sion analysis, is characterized by a peak at the beginning with a rapid decline thereafter. This life cycle pattern is sharply contradicted by the evidence of drug life cycles in the present study that indicates a gradual increase over several years followed by stabilization.

Estimates of the average internal rate of return of six pharmaceutical firms were also made by Stauffer.[18] These are presented in table 11. Stauffer's estimates cannot be compared directly with the estimates of the internal rate of return in the present study since his six firms were not intended to be representative of the entire pharmaceutical industry. Stauffer's main purpose, in fact, was to illustrate the serious bias that may result from the use of an accounting rate of return as a measure of the internal rate of return. He points out the many crucial assumptions made in his estimation technique that may bias the estimate of the internal rate of return.

Schwartzman estimated the internal rate of return for drugs whose R & D was carried out in 1973 and in 1960.[19] He concluded that the upper limit of the internal rate of return in 1973 was 3.3 percent, and the lower limit of the internal rate of return in 1960 was 11.4 percent. Lack of sufficient data prevented Schwartzman from calculating an estimate of the rate of return itself. Instead he calculated an upper limit of the 1973 rate of return through the use of assumptions that are likely to bias the estimate upward.

Schwartzman's method may be briefly summarized as follows. He compiled a list of significant NCE drugs introduced annually in the United States. During 1966–1972, an average of 12.3 such drugs were introduced annually. The average R & D cost per NCE drug was estimated to be $24.4 million, in 1973 dollars. This estimate was arrived at by excluding from the total R & D cost those costs that are not attributable to significant NCE

TABLE 12
Cash Flows of an Average NCE Drug
(millions of dollars)

Year	R & D Cost	Year	Net Income
1	1.22	11	0.47
2	1.22	12	0.94
3	1.22	13	1.40
4	1.22	14	1.40
5	1.22	15	1.40
6	1.22	16	1.40
7	1.22	17	1.40
8	1.22	18	1.40
9	1.22	19	1.40
10	1.22	20	1.40
		21	1.40
		22	1.40
		23	1.40
		24	0.94
		25	0.47

Source: Schwartzman, *The Expected Return from Pharmaceutical Research,* table 8.

drugs, and dividing the total cost by the number of NCE drugs. The after-tax cost per NCE drug, assuming a 50 percent tax rate, is $12.2 million. The R & D period for a significant NCE drug was assumed to be ten years, with R & D expenditures uniformly distributed during the period.

To estimate income from NCE drug sales, Schwartzman computed an after-tax profit margin on sales of 12.8 percent. He also estimated the total annual sales per NCE at $11 million, which yields a net cash inflow of $1.4 million when the profit margin is applied. A fifteen-year life cycle is assumed, including increasing, stable, and decreasing stages. The cash flows are represented in table 12.

Applying the discounted-cash-flows formula to these amounts, Schwartzman concluded that the expected rate of return on R & D performed in 1973 was 3.3 percent. Schwartzman also argued that the assumptions used to arrive at the cash-flow estimates are such that this rate of return is an upper limit of the rate of return, rather than an estimate of the rate of return itself. Using a similar method, Schwartzman concluded that the lower limit on the estimate of the internal rate of return of R & D performed in 1960 is 11.4 percent.

Examination of the results shows that Schwartzman's estimate for 1960 is not in conflict with the estimates in this study because the lower limit figure of 11.4 percent provided by Schwartzman is indeed lower than the internal rate of return estimated in this study for drugs introduced throughout the 1960s. Schwartzman's estimate of the rate of return for 1973, however, is subject to a number of assumptions that may account for a serious downward bias, a bias opposite to the one desired by Schwartzman.

One such bias relates to the estimate of the length of the life cycle of drugs. Schwartzman used Clymer's estimate of fifteen years.[20] Data presented in this study, however, show that the average drug life cycle is more than double Schwartzman's figure. A second bias results from the exclusion of combination drugs by Schwartzman. Combination drugs are byproducts of NCE drugs. They require relatively little R & D expenditures, and their sales revenues are significant, as can be seen in table 5. If the rate of return on combination drugs is higher than that on NCE drugs, then excluding combination drugs will bias the estimated rate of return downward. As stated earlier, a separation of combination drugs from NCE drugs for the purpose of rate of return estimation is not valid since they are in fact one product.

Lastly, Schwartzman's estimate of the profit margin on NCE drugs is assumed to be identical to the average profit margin on all sales of pharmaceutical firms. Pharmaceutical firms sell more than NCE drugs, however. A study by Arthur D. Little, Inc., shows that the profit margin on pharmaceuticals is considerably higher than the profit margin on the other products that many pharmaceutical firms produce and sell.[21] Using an average profit margin of pharmaceuticals and nonpharmaceuticals, as Schwartzman did, imparts a downward bias to the profit margin and to the resulting estimate of the rate of return.

The studies by Baily, Stauffer, and Schwartzman differ in their estimation procedures of the rate of return. It is important to note, however, that their estimates of the return for the late 1960s and the 1970s are all considerably lower than the accounting rate of return for the industry. This general result receives further confirmation in this study.

Notes

1. W. E. Cox reported a median life cycle of five years for NCE drugs, in "Product Life Cycles and Promotional Strategy in the Ethical Drugs Industry" (unpublished dissertation, University of Michigan, 1963). Cox's definition of a drug is narrower than the definition used here. Cox defined a drug as having a particular dosage form and a particular potency. The definition used here aggregates over all dosage forms and potencies. In addition, the length of the life cycle of the average drug, as defined here, is equal to the maximum length of the life cycles of individual drugs of a given group. This period will usually be longer than the median life as reported by Cox.

2. The estimation of the parameters of the life cycle is presented in appendix A.

3. See appendix A.

34

4. If, for example, in a given year ten NCE drugs and twenty combination drugs were introduced, a drug "unit" will include one NCE drug and two combination drugs. A precise definition of a drug unit would require an identification of NCE drugs which each combination drug is composed of and the attribution of a share of the combination drug to each relevant NCE drug. This method, however, is not practical, and the definition used is an approximation.

5. Arthur D. Little, Inc., *Prospects for U.S. Health Care Companies, 1975–1977* (Cambridge, Mass.: Arthur D. Little, Inc., 1975).

6. For a discussion of this point, see E. Solomon and J. J. Pringle, *An Introduction to Financial Management* (Santa Monica, Calif.: Goodyear Publishing Co., Inc., 1977), chap. 11.

7. The internal rate of return is computed in a framework where expenditures equal to Dep_E are made annually to maintain the capital stock at its original value, so the salvage value of capital is equal to its original value. See footnote 2.

8. It is possible that the accounting measure of depreciation is different from the economic measure, although the exact magnitude of the difference is difficult to estimate. In this case, the method used here will introduce a bias in the profit margin and in the estimate of the internal rate of return. The ratio of depreciation to sales revenue in the pharmaceutical industry, however, is only approximately 3 percent, and any resulting bias will be small.

9. Arthur D. Little, Inc., *Prospects for U.S. Health Care Companies*. The estimates in Arthur D. Little are for the period of the mid-1970s. Profit margins in the industry, however, were fairly stable over the period 1954–1978 (Citibank, *Monthly Economic Letter*, New York (various issues).

10. These proportions were estimated as the average proportions in a sample of ethical drug firms. Data were obtained from *Compustat* tapes.

11. Arthur D. Little, Inc., provides data on profit margins on domestic sales only. No direct estimates of the profit margin on exports were available. It was assumed that the profit margin on exports of ethical drugs is identical to that on domestic sales.

12. The estimation methodology is presented in appendix B.

13. The estimation methodology is presented in appendix B.

14. Analysis of foreign markets is presented in appendix C.

15. M. N. Baily, "Research and Development Costs and Returns: The U.S. Pharmaceutical Industry," *Journal of Political Economy*, vol. 80 (January–February 1972), pp. 70–85. The estimated cash flows into R & D and from sales are combined in a discounted-cash-flow model to yield estimates of the rate of return. The R & D function is of the form $N_t/E_t = f(D_t, P_t)$, where N_t = number of NCE drugs introduced in year t, E_t = R & D expenditures that become effective in year t (an average of R & D expenditures in years $t - 4$, $t - 5$, and $t - 6$), D_t = dummy variable separating the pre-1962 amendment to the Food, Drugs, and Cosmetics Act from the following period, P_t = a measure of depletion of research opportunities.

The returns function is of the form $t/Z_t = g(N_t \ldots N_{t-17})$, where t = sales revenue minus manufacturing costs, and Z_t = market size.

16. The tax rate is from Arthur D. Little, Inc., *Prospects for U.S. Health Care Companies*.

17. H. G. Grabowski, *Drug Regulation and Innovation* (Washington, D.C.: American Enterprise Institute, 1976), p. 26.

18. T. R. Stauffer, "Profitability Measures in the Pharmaceutical Industry," in *Drug Development and Marketing*, ed. R. B. Helms (Washington, D.C.: American Enterprise Institute, 1975), pp. 97–119.

19. D. Schwartzman, *The Expected Return from Pharmaceutical Research* (Washington, D.C.: American Enterprise Institute, 1975).

20. H. A. Clymer, "The Economics of Drug Innovation," in *The Development and Control of New Drug Products*, ed. M. Pernarowski and M. Darrach (Vancouver, B.C.: Evergreen Press, 1971), pp. 109–29.

21. Arthur D. Little, Inc., *Prospects for U.S. Health Care Companies*, table 3.

5
The Cost of Capital in the U.S. Ethical Pharmaceutical Industry

As we saw in chapter 3, a comparison over time of the cost of capital with the expected average internal rate of return of a firm can be used to measure monopoly power or to trace the temporary divergences of an industry from a long-run competitive equilibrium. Chapter 4 provided estimates of the average internal rate of return in the ethical pharmaceutical industry. This chapter provides estimates of the cost of capital.

The cost of capital to the ethical pharmaceutical industry is estimated as a market-value-weighted average of the cost of capital to a representative sample of ethical pharmaceutical firms.[1] The cost of capital to individual firms is estimated as a market-value-weighted average of the cost of the components of the capital structure.[2] The capital structure of a firm is composed of four elements: common stock, preferred stock, long-term debt, and short-term debt.

We shall first estimate the cost of each of the components of the capital structure. These costs are already adjusted to account for the particular level of risk that typifies ethical pharmaceutical operation. A discussion of the measurement of risk in the ethical pharmaceutical industry is presented in appendix D. Finally, we shall present the weighted average cost of capital in the ethical pharmaceutical industry.

The Cost of Equity Capital (Common Stock)

The cost of equity is the minimum rate of return that must be earned on the equity-financed portion of the capital structure so as not to cause a decline in the market value of a firm's stock. Using the Capital Asset Pricing Model,[3] we can express the cost of equity capital of firm j as:

$$E(R_j) = R_f + [E(R_m) - R_f] \beta_j$$

where
$E(R_j)$ = the cost of equity capital of firm j,
R_f = the risk-free rate,
$E(R_m)$ = the expected return for the market portfolio

TABLE 13
Beta Values and Market Values
for Twelve Ethical Pharmaceutical Firms

Firm	Adjusted Beta Value	Market Value of Common Stock ($ millions)
Abbott	1.14	1,672
Lilly	1.01	2,673
Merck	1.04	4,193
Pfizer	1.11	1,924
Rorer-Amchem	1.04	220
Schering-Plough	1.06	1,616
Searle	1.12	664
SmithKline	1.00	1,491
Squibb	1.17	1,066
Syntex	0.95	401
Upjohn	0.65	1,060
Warner-Lambert	1.23	2,065

Sources: Betas are from Merrill Lynch, Pierce, Fenner and Smith, Inc., *Security Risk Evaluation* (New York: Merrill Lynch, April 1977). Market values of common stock are the December 31, 1977, values obtained from *Compustat* tapes.

β_j = the change in the expected return on stock j relative to the change in the return on the market portfolio

The Risk Premium. Roger Ibbotson and Rex Sinquefield analyzed the annual returns from securities over the period 1926–1978.[4] They used the annual returns on Standard and Poor's 500-stock index as a measure of the return on the market portfolio, R_m. The return on long-term government bonds can be used as a measure of the risk-free rate, R_f.[5] The risk premium $[E(R_m) - R_f]$ is defined as the difference between the expected return on the market portfolio and the risk-free rate. The risk premium was estimated here as the difference between the average rate of return on common stock and the average rate of return for long-term government bonds over the period 1926–1978. The risk premium turns out to be 11.2 − 3.4, or 7.8 percent.

Beta Values. Beta values, the β_j's of the Capital Asset Pricing Model, for individual firms are computed and published by a number of sources. Betas published by Merrill Lynch were used here.[6] These betas are computed by using Standard and Poor's 500-stock index as a measure of the market portfolio. Betas and market values of the common stock of twelve pharmaceutical companies are presented in table 13.[7] The market-value-weighted average beta for the pharmaceutical industry was estimated to be 1.06.[8]

TABLE 14
THE RISK-FREE RATE OF RETURN, COST OF EQUITY CAPITAL (COMMON STOCK), AND COST OF PREFERRED STOCK IN THE ETHICAL PHARMACEUTICAL INDUSTRY, 1951–1977
(percent)

Year	Risk-Free Rate of Return	Cost of Equity Capital[a]	Cost of Preferred Stock
1951	2.57	10.84	4.82
1952	2.68	10.95	4.88
1953	2.94	11.21	5.12
1954	2.55	10.82	4.75
1955	2.84	11.11	4.49
1956	3.08	11.35	4.74
1957	3.47	11.74	5.28
1958	3.43	11.70	5.14
1959	4.07	12.34	4.99
1960	4.01	12.28	5.18
1961	3.90	12.17	4.82
1962	3.95	12.22	4.81
1963	4.00	12.27	4.69
1964	4.15	12.42	4.67
1965	4.21	12.48	4.60
1966	4.65	12.92	5.03
1967	4.85	13.12	5.34
1968	5.26	13.53	5.83
1969	7.12	15.39	6.62
1970	6.53	14.80	7.70
1971	5.70	13.97	7.11
1972	5.54	13.81	7.03
1973	6.21	14.48	7.29
1974	6.88	15.15	8.37
1975	6.96	15.23	8.47
1976	6.79	15.06	7.92
1977	7.53	15.80	7.79

a. Calculated using the equation $E(R_j) = R_f + [E(R_m) - R_f] \beta_j$, with estimates of the risk-free rate, the market risk premium, and beta.

SOURCES: The risk-free rate of return is estimated as the average yield to maturity on long-term U.S. bonds reported in *Moody's Municipal and Government Manual*, 1979. Medium-grade industrial preferred stocks (see *Moody's Industrial Manual*, 1979, p. a42) are the basis for measuring the cost of preferred stock.

The Risk-Free Rate. The risk-free rate, R_f, was estimated as the average yield to maturity on long-term government bonds issued in a given year.[9] These rates are presented in table 14. The data on the risk-free rate, beta, and the risk premium can now be incorporated into the Capital Asset

TABLE 15
BOND RATINGS AND LONG-TERM DEBT
OF TWELVE ETHICAL PHARMACEUTICAL FIRMS, 1965, 1970, 1975

Firm	Moody's Bond Ratings	Long-Term Debt Outstanding ($ millions) 1975	1970	1965
Abbott	Aa	215	47	5
Lilly	n.a.	12	5	0
Merck	Aaa	219	18	0
Pfizer	Aa	472	48	30
Rorer-Amchem	n.a.	2	1	0
Schering-Plough	n.a.	3	4	0
Searle	Aa	347	49	0
SmithKline	Aa	101	0	0
Squibb	Aa	273	120	3
Syntex	n.a.	42	0	0
Upjohn	Aa	181	22	0
Warner-Lambert	Aaa	262	51	0

n.a. = not available.
SOURCE: *Moody's Industrial Manual*, 1976, and Standard and Poor, *Compustat*, New York, 1976.

Pricing Model to yield estimates of the cost of equity capital for the twelve sample firms. The estimates for the period 1951–1977 are presented in table 14.

The Cost of Preferred Stock

The cost of preferred stock was assumed to be equal to the average yield on medium-grade industrial preferred stock and is presented in table 14.[10]

The Cost of Long-Term Debt

Moody's Industrial Manual, 1976, provides ratings of bonds of eight out of the twelve ethical pharmaceutical firms in our sample. The remaining four firms had little or no long-term debt outstanding in 1975. Table 15 presents Moody's ratings of long-term debt of the sample firms.

With the exception of Merck and Warner-Lambert, which have an Aaa rating, all firms for which ratings are available have an Aa rating. Thus, the average yield on Aa industrial bonds was used as an estimate of the cost of long-term debt and is presented in table 16.[11]

TABLE 16

COST OF SHORT-TERM AND LONG-TERM DEBT IN THE ETHICAL PHARMACEUTICAL INDUSTRY, 1951–1977

(percent)

Year	Cost of Long-Term Debt	Cost of Short-Term Debt
1951	2.82	2.17
1952	2.93	2.33
1953	3.23	2.52
1954	3.02	1.59
1955	3.11	2.21
1956	3.39	3.31
1957	3.89	3.82
1958	3.78	2.47
1959	4.36	3.97
1960	4.39	3.85
1961	4.33	2.96
1962	4.30	3.26
1963	4.29	3.56
1964	4.41	3.96
1965	4.50	4.38
1966	5.15	5.55
1967	5.55	5.11
1968	6.24	5.90
1969	7.05	7.83
1970	7.94	7.72
1971	7.23	5.11
1972	7.11	4.50
1973	7.40	6.54
1974	8.64	7.81
1975	8.90	6.21
1976	8.59	5.35
1977	8.04	5.60

SOURCES: The cost of long-term debt is based on the average yield on Aa industrial bonds in *Moody's Industrial Manual*, 1979, p. a39. Data for the cost of short-term debt are from Standard and Poor, *Statistical Service, Current Statistics*, New York (various issues).

The Cost of Short-Term Debt

The cost of short-term debt was assumed to be equal to the average yield on commercial paper (Prime, four to six months).[12] It is presented in table 16.

TABLE 17
WEIGHTED AVERAGE CAPITAL STRUCTURE OF TWELVE PHARMACEUTICAL FIRMS, 1961–1977
(percent)

Year	Common Stock	Preferred Stock	Long-Term Debt	Short-Term Debt
1961	98.6	0.3	0.6	0.5
1962	97.9	1.0	0.6	0.5
1963	98.6	0.6	0.3	0.5
1964	98.6	0.6	0.4	0.4
1965	98.8	0.4	0.3	0.5
1966	97.0	1.6	0.7	0.7
1967	96.5	1.3	1.1	1.1
1968	96.7	1.0	1.5	0.8
1969	96.6	0.8	1.6	1.0
1970	95.3	1.0	1.9	1.8
1971	95.8	0.3	1.9	2.0
1972	96.2	0.2	2.2	1.4
1973	95.1	0.1	2.9	1.9
1974	91.4	0.1	4.9	3.6
1975	88.3	0.1	8.3	3.3
1976	80.7	0.0	15.6	3.7
1977	85.1	0.0	9.6	5.2

SOURCE: Standard and Poor, *Compustat*, New York.

The Cost of Capital in the Ethical Pharmaceutical Industry

The cost of capital of each firm can be computed as a weighted average of the costs of the components of the capital structure.[13] Using a marginal corporate tax of 48 percent, we may define the after-tax cost of capital as being equal to $0.52(W_lL + W_sS) + W_cC + W_pP$, where L = the cost of long-term debt, S = the cost of short-term debt, C = the cost of equity capital (common stock), P = the cost of preferred stock, and W_l, W_s, W_c, and W_p are the weights of the corresponding components in the capital structure. The weights of the components of the capital structure are proportional to their market value.[14] The market value of common stock of each sample firm was computed by multiplying the number of common shares outstanding by the price per share.[15]

Data on the market value of preferred stock were not available. Consequently, the book value of this stock was used as an estimate. Because there was a generally increasing trend in preferred stock yields during 1951–

TABLE 18
Weighted Average After-Tax Cost of Capital
of Twelve Ethical Pharmaceutical Firms, 1951–1977
(percent)

Year	Cost of Capital
1951	10.72
1952	10.82
1953	11.08
1954	10.69
1955	10.98
1956	11.22
1957	11.61
1958	11.57
1959	12.20
1960	12.15
1961	12.03
1962	12.03
1963	12.14
1964	12.29
1965	12.37
1966	12.65
1967	12.79
1968	13.21
1969	15.02
1970	14.33
1971	13.53
1972	13.41
1973	13.95
1974	14.22
1975	13.95
1976	12.95
1977	14.00

Source: Computed on basis of data in tables 13, 14, 16, and 17.

1977, we may expect that the market value of preferred stock is generally lower than its book value. As shown in table 17, however, the weight of preferred stock in the capital structure of the sample firms, even when measured at book value, is negligible. Any bias resulting from the use of book value here will be small, and no attempt was made to correct for it. Since the market value of short-term debt is identical to its book value, no bias is introduced by the use of book value of short-term debt as a measure of market value.

The use of book value of long-term debt as a measure of market value is susceptible to the same type of error that was discussed for preferred stock since long-term interest rates have generally increased during 1951–1977. Significant use of long-term debt by the sample firms is a fairly recent phenomenon, however, as can be seen from table 15. Also, table 16 indicates that long-term interest rates did not vary considerably between 1970 and 1975, the period during which most of the long-term debt was acquired. Thus, the market value of such debt should be fairly close to its book value, which was used as an estimate. The weighted average capital structure of the sample firms is presented in table 17.[16]

The weighted average cost of capital of the sample firms, which serves as our estimate of the cost of capital in the ethical pharmaceutical industry, is presented in table 18. The relevant cost of capital for a drug introduced in a given year is the cost of capital at the year when the R & D project leading to that drug was started, because this is when the investment decision is made. The R & D program for drugs introduced in 1956, for example, started, on average, in 1952 (see table 10) and the cost of capital for that year was 10.8 percent. The cost of capital for drugs introduced each year during 1954–1978 is presented in table 2.

Notes

1. The twelve ethical pharmaceutical firms in the sample are: Abbott, Lilly, Merck, Pfizer, Rorer-Amchem, Schering-Plough, Searle, SmithKline, Squibb, Syntex, Upjohn, and Warner-Lambert. In 1975 the sample firms ranked among the top twenty-eight firms in the ethical pharmaceutical industry when ranked according to domestic ethical drugs sales. The top twenty-eight firms accounted for 83 percent of domestic ethical drugs sales in 1975 and are a good representation of the group of firms that devote significant efforts to drug innovation. As noted in chapter 1, this is the group of firms that this study focuses on. (Data on sales are from IMS America, Ltd., *U.S. Pharmaceutical Market, Drug Stores and Hospitals* [Ambler, Pa.: IMS, 1975].)

2. See J. C. Van Horne, *Financial Management and Policy*, 4th ed. (Englewood Cliffs, N.J.: Prentice-Hall, 1977), p. 209.

3. An analysis of the model may be found in W. F. Sharpe, *Portfolio Theory and Capital Markets* (New York: McGraw-Hill, 1970).

4. R. G. Ibbotson and R. A. Sinquefield, "Stocks, Bonds, Bills and Inflation: Updates," *Financial Analysts Journal* (July–August 1979), pp. 40–44.

5. The return on long-term bonds rather than the return on short-term bills is the appropriate measure of the risk-free rate in this case because the investment projects that we are evaluating are long-term projects.

6. Merrill Lynch, Pierce, Fenner and Smith, Inc., *Security Risk Evaluation* (New York: Merrill Lynch, April 1977).

7. Market values of common stock at the end of each year were obtained from *Compustat* tapes.

8. Using data over 1947–1975, Chien and Upson estimated beta of the Standard and Poor sample of the pharmaceutical industry as 0.94. They also estimated beta over six partial periods. Although the estimated beta over shorter periods varied, there was no obvious trend. See Robert I. Chien and Roger B. Upson, "Returns to Drug Industry Common Stock: An Alternative Measure of Economic Profitability," *Managerial and Decision Economics*, vol. 1, no. 4 (1980), pp. 172–78.

9. Moody's Investors Service, Inc., *Moody's Municipal and Government Manual* (New York, 1979), p. a6.

10. *Moody's Industrial Manual*, 1979, p. a42.

11. Ibid., p. a39.

12. Standard and Poor, *Statistical Service, Current Statistics*, New York (various issues).

13. A number of assumptions are implied here. For a discussion, see Van Horne, *Financial Management and Policy*, chap. 8.

14. Data on the capital structure was derived from *Compustat* tapes.

15. Price per share used is the price on December 31 of each year. Data are from the *Compustat* tapes.

16. This is a weighted average in which the total market value of each firm serves as a weight. Complete data for the period prior to 1961 were not available, and 1961 weights were used for the 1951–1960 period.

6
Competition in the U.S. Ethical Pharmaceutical Industry

According to Joseph Califano, former secretary of health, education, and welfare, "there is precious little competition among pharmaceutical companies.... For pharmaceutical companies ... research has become big business, with patent monopoly pots of gold at the end of the research rainbow."[1]

Chapters 4 and 5 of this study presented evidence on the declining profitability of investment in pharmaceutical research and development. The evidence on the return to R & D in recent years contradicts the assertion that monopoly profits exist in the pharmaceutical industry. As summarized in table 2, the expected average return is lower than the cost of capital, or normal return. This chapter will examine the evidence on the wider issue of the competitive behavior of the pharmaceutical industry.

Concentration and Competition

Industry concentration is often used to measure monopoly power. If we apply this measure to the ethical pharmaceutical industry we note that the industry is not highly concentrated. In 1972 the four largest and the eight largest firms of the pharmaceutical preparation industry accounted for 26 and 44 percent, respectively, of the value of industry shipments. The four-firm concentration ratio of 26 percent places the pharmaceutical industry at the 36th percentile of all industries, well below the median.[2] Examining the concentration in the pharmaceutical industry over time, we note no particular trend during the period 1947–1972 for the four-firm and eight-firm concentration indices (see table 19).

Although the concentration ratio of the pharmaceutical industry is lower than the median concentration ratio for all industries, it does not necessarily imply that monopoly power is absent. Even if we accept the view that firms in industries with low concentration ratios have no control over prices, it is not clear at which level of concentration monopoly power begins. The Hart bill contains a presumption of monopoly power if the four-firm concentration level exceeds 50 percent; the Neal Committee

TABLE 19
CONCENTRATION RATIOS IN THE PHARMACEUTICAL PREPARATIONS INDUSTRY, 1947–1972

| Year | Value of Industry Shipments (percent accounted for by): | |
	Four largest companies	Eight largest companies
1947	28	44
1954	25	44
1958	27	45
1963	22	38
1966	24	41
1967	24	40
1970	26	43
1972	26	44

SOURCE: U.S. Bureau of the Census, 1972 Census of Manufacturers, Concentration Ratios in Manufacturing, MC72(SR)-2, Washington, D.C., 1975, table 5.

suggested 70 percent, and Kaysen and Turner suggested 80 percent.[3]

It has been argued that the relatively low industry-wide concentration ratio of the pharmaceutical industry is not pertinent to the question of monopoly power because the pharmaceutical market is naturally separable into individual therapeutic markets. Drugs in different therapeutic classes are poor substitutes for one another.[4] When measured within therapeutic markets, concentration in the pharmaceutical industry increases substantially as shown in table 20.

Although the data in table 20 present four-firm concentration ratios that are considerably higher than the overall concentration ratios presented in table 19, these ratios cannot be interpreted unless comparable separation of markets is performed for nonpharmaceutical markets as well. William Shepherd adjusted industry concentration measures to account for the effects of the existence of distinct regional markets, noncompeting products within a given industry, and the level of imports. He found that the average adjusted concentration ratio for 1966 was 60.3 percent, which is more than 50 percent higher than the average raw census concentration ratio of 39.0 percent. Shepherd indicates that care was taken not to overstate the adjusted estimates, so it is likely that the figure of 60.3 percent is biased downward.[5] It is clear that the difference between raw and adjusted concentration ratios is substantial. Still, Shepherd admits that many of the adjustments can only be rough approximations. Thus, the need to adjust

TABLE 20
CONCENTRATION RATIOS IN MAJOR THERAPEUTIC
MARKETS, 1972

Therapeutic Market	Market Share of Top Four Firms (percent)
Analgesics	60
Antacids	86
Antibacterials	80
Antibiotics (broad and medium spectrum)	60
Antihistamines	59
Antiobesity products	83
Antispasmodics	57
Ataraxics and tranquilizers	76
Cardiovasculars	54
Diabetic therapy	76
Diuretics	74
Muscle relaxants	50
Oral contraceptives	86
Psychostimulants	85
Sedatives	46
Sulfonamides	81

SOURCE: Arthur D. Little, Inc., *The Pharmaceutical Industry: An Analysis of 1973 Sales and an Assessment of Current Products* (Cambridge, Mass.: Arthur D. Little, Inc., 1974).

concentration ratios presents another major drawback for the use of concentration ratios as measures of monopoly power.

The concentration ratios of individual therapeutic markets, as presented in table 20, are still generally higher than the average adjusted concentration ratio of 60.3 percent, although the exact difference depends upon the extent to which the average adjusted concentration ratio is biased downward. Douglas Cocks and John Virts, however, provide evidence that shows that the boundaries of therapeutic markets as defined by marketing research firms are narrower than the true boundaries of the relevant economic markets constructed according to measures of cross-elasticity of substitution of drugs.[6] Thus, it is likely that the concentration ratios that are based upon therapeutic markets defined on the present basis are biased upward, and the difference between the average adjusted concentration ratio and concentration ratios in the therapeutic markets may be even lower than previously indicated.

47

Barriers to Entry and Competition

The rationale behind the use of concentration ratios as a measure of monopoly power is that high concentration is presumed to be a necessary condition for collusive behavior of the firms in an industry. Collusion allows prices to exceed marginal cost, and profits to exceed normal profits. The ability to collude, however, depends upon the ease of entry of firms into the market. If entry is easy, then the expectation of long-run profits in excess of normal profits will draw firms into the market, causing prices to decline until excess profits are eliminated. Although Joe Bain has recognized that a theory of oligopoly cannot be complete without the element of barriers to entry,[7] Harold Demsetz correctly points out that the interpretation of concentration ratios as measures of monopoly power ignores the possibility of entry.[8] Thus, the use of concentration ratios as a measure of monopoly power without measurement of barriers to entry may be misleading. The measurement of barriers to entry, however, presents problems that may be more complicated than those associated with the measurement of concentration ratios.

William Comanor argues that by means of barriers to entry pharmaceutical companies are able to achieve and maintain high concentration ratios in therapeutic markets:

> The crucial significance of product differentiation is that it provides the primary barrier to entry into the relevant therapeutic markets. Since effective entry normally requires some form of technical advance, the cost and risk of research compromise an important part of this barrier. Joined with research and development, moreover, are the extremely high selling expenditures undertaken by larger firms.... Entry barriers, created in this fashion, have resulted in fairly high levels of concentration within therapeutic markets.[9]

It may be true that the costs of R & D and promotion keep those small pharmaceutical firms that are currently providing nonpatented drugs under generic names from entering certain markets. These firms do not possess the expertise needed for R & D and promotion and are unlikely to acquire the resources that are needed for significant entry into therapeutic markets unless profits are very attractive.

Entry, however, need not necessarily be by new firms or small firms. Effective entry may be achieved by large firms that operate in fields other than pharmaceuticals, as well as by established pharmaceutical firms entering new therapeutic markets. An example of the first type of entry is 3M Company's venture into the field of pharmaceuticals through its acquisition of Rikers Laboratories. The second type of entry, however, is much more significant. Although substitution in consumption between

TABLE 21

FIRM TURNOVER FOR THE LEADING TWENTY-ONE FIRMS
IN THE ETHICAL PHARMACEUTICAL INDUSTRY, 1962 AND 1972

	\multicolumn{3}{c}{Rank in Terms of Market Share}		
Firm	1962	1972	Change in rank
Lilly	1	1	0
Hoffmann-LaRoche	10	2	8
American Home Products	3	3	0
Merck	6	4	2
Bristol-Myers	13	5	8
Abbott	11	6	5
Pfizer	12	7	5
Ciba-Geigy	8	8	0
Upjohn	4	9	−5
Squibb	9	10	−1
SmithKline	2	11	−9
Johnson & Johnson	22	12	10
Schering-Plough	15	13	2
Parke-Davis	7	14	−7
Searle	17	15	2
Lederle	5	16	−11
Sandoz-Wander	19	17	2
Robins	18	18	0
Sterling	16	19	−3
Burroughs Wellcome	20	20	0
Warner-Lambert	14	21	−7
Average absolute change in rank between 1962 and 1972			4.1

SOURCE: Cocks, "Product Innovation and the Dynamic Elements of Competition in the Ethical Pharmaceutical Industry."

products in different therapeutic markets is not usual, substitution on the production side is not nearly as difficult.

Lester Telser analyzed entry of pharmaceutical firms into therapeutic markets new to them and found that price levels declined in response to entry.[10] Douglas Cocks found that the pharmaceutical industry is ranked second among all industries according to market share instability.[11] The changes in market position due to entry are considerable, as can be seen in table 21, and this instability casts much doubt upon the argument that the high concentration ratios in the pharmaceutical industry, as measured in the individual therapeutic fields, indicate collusive behavior.

One way to determine whether barriers to entry exist in a market is to look at actual entry. If a monopolistic firm expects entry, however, it may reduce prices to levels where profits are no more than normal profits, producing an output that is equal to the one that would be achieved under perfect competition. In such a case, monopoly power may not exist even when concentration ratios are high and where there is no actual entry. A meaningful measure of barriers to entry must rely on potential entry rather than actual entry. Significant entry in the pharmaceutical industry can occur only as a result of the introduction of new drugs, which in turn depends upon R & D projects that a firm conducts.

The path leading from R & D programs to actual drug innovations, however, is uncertain. Research in a particular area may take a little longer or settle on a less satisfactory solution than research done by competitors. The fact that we observe only a few firms in a particular therapeutic category tells us little about how many firms are trying to get in and how many were only nearly as successful. Thus, the actual level of market entry that is reflected in the market share instability presented in table 21 is a downward-biased measure of the relevant measure of entry. Table 22 presents some data on the extent of potential entry of eighteen major pharmaceutical firms into therapeutic markets where they had no sales in 1972.[12]

The data in table 22 reveal that, on average, there were almost five major firms that were attempting to enter each of the therapeutic markets where they had no representation in 1972. This potential entry places a limit on the exercise of monopoly power by firms that hold significant shares of each therapeutic market.

Price and Quality Competition

The theory of administered prices, developed by Gardiner Means, states that firms possessing monopoly power can set their prices almost independently of the market forces of supply and demand.[13] Means supported his theory with evidence of rigidity in prices of products sold by concentrated industries. Similar evidence was presented by Jesse Markham, who found evidence for the administered price hypothesis in the pharmaceutical industry.[14] The prices of more than 50 percent of his sample of 308 drugs did not change at all during the period 1949–1959. When prices did change, it was usually because of new packaging or a new dosage form. Additional evidence of price rigidity of drugs was presented by Henry Steele and Peter Costello.[15]

Cocks and Virts tested the administered price hypothesis in the pharmaceutical industry correcting for two problems in Markham's study. Markham used catalog prices, not transaction prices. Cocks and Virts used

TABLE 22

THE NUMBER OF MAJOR PHARMACEUTICAL FIRMS THAT CONDUCTED R & D AIMED AT DRUG INNOVATION IN THERAPEUTIC FIELDS WHERE THEY HAD NO MARKET SHARE, 1972

Therapeutic Field	No. of Firms[a]
Analgesics	6
Antacids	3
Antiarthritics	5
Antibacterials	4
Antibiotics (broad and medium spectrum)	4
Antihistamines	7
Antiobesity	3
Antispasmodics	4
Ataraxics	7
Cardiovasculars	8
Corticoids	2
Diabetic therapy	5
Diuretics	2
Muscle relaxants	5
Oral contraceptives	8
Psychostimulants	11
Sedatives	1
Sulfonamides	3
Average number of firms	4.9

a. This is the number of firms out of a group of eighteen firms.
SOURCE: Data on market shares are from Arthur D. Little, Inc., *The Pharmaceutical Industry: An Analysis of 1973 Sales and an Assessment of Current Products* (Cambridge, Mass.: Arthur D. Little, 1974). Data on R & D activity are from the Stanford Research Institute, *The U.S. Health Products Market to 1980* (Menlo Park, Calif.: Stanford Research Institute, 1973), Appendix F.

actual prices paid instead of catalog prices. Also, they adjusted prices to reflect changes in the size of prescription.[16] As table 23 shows, Cocks and Virts found that prices of drugs exhibited considerable volatility, a finding that undermines the administered price hypothesis.

W. Duncan Reekie investigated the pricing of new drugs to test the hypothesis that prices of drugs are not affected by their quality, because doctors are targets of much advertising, but do not pay for drugs that they choose for their patients.[17] Reekie recorded the prices of new drugs relative to prices of existing drugs in a given therapeutic field. As can be seen in table 24, drugs with high therapeutic gain were more likely to be priced above the average price of existing drugs than drugs with low therapeutic gain. This result contradicts the hypothesis that physicians choose drugs without regard to prices.

TABLE 23

Price Indexes of Leading Products in Ten Ethical-Drug Product Sets, 1962–1971
(1962 = 100)

Product Set	1962	1963	1964	1965	1966	1967	1968	1969	1970	1971
Vitamin and hematinic	100	100.3	98.5	97.4	97.4	97.2	97.1	100.4	101.3	101.3
Anti-infective	100	92.8	90.4	87.9	84.9	77.6	74.8	73.7	71.3	68.2
Cough and cold	100	107.0	101.6	99.9	99.7	99.5	99.9	104.5	105.7	108.3
Analgesic and anti-inflammatory	100	100.7	100.0	103.0	99.0	97.5	95.7	96.3	95.6	98.0
Antihypertensive and diuretic	100	98.4	97.4	97.2	96.1	95.8	93.1	91.4	92.3	93.4
Psychopharmaceutical	100	99.4	97.7	96.3	95.3	94.8	91.6	93.4	92.2	91.7
Antiobesity	100	103.1	101.4	100.8	99.2	99.7	98.6	100.2	101.3	105.1
Oral contraceptive	100	85.9	79.7	76.3	75.5	70.6	69.1	73.0	75.3	77.0
Anticholinergic and antispasmodic	100	101.2	99.8	99.8	99.9	98.8	99.0	99.1	101.0	100.7
Diabetic therapy	100	95.7	89.0	87.1	83.8	81.7	82.3	81.6	80.3	81.0
BLS[a] consumer price index for prescriptions	100	97.6	96.3	95.2	95.1	93.4	91.8	93.0	94.5	94.6
BLS[a] consumer price index for all goods	100	101.2	102.5	104.3	107.3	110.4	115.0	121.2	128.4	133.9

a. BLS = Bureau of Labor Statistics.
SOURCE: Cocks and Virts, "Pricing Behavior of the Pharmaceutical Industry," table 5.

TABLE 24
New Chemical Entities Analyzed by Price and by Food and Drug Administration Rating, 1958–1975

Relative Price (P_{NCE}/P_c)	FDA Rating Criteria			
	Important therapeutic gain[a]	Modest therapeutic gain[b]	Little or no therapeutic gain[c]	Total
Less than 1.0	7(10%)	12(17%)	53(73%)	72(100%)
From 1.0 to 1.5	6(10%)	13(20%)	44(70%)	63(100%)
Greater than 1.5	16(44%)	9(25%)	11(31%)	36(100%)
Total	29(17%)	34(20%)	108(63%)	171(100%)

NOTES: All data refer to date of product introduction.

P_{NCE} = dollar sales of the new chemical entity (NCE) made through new prescriptions divided by numbers of new prescriptions written for the NCE—that is, average price of a new prescription for the NCE (in terms of dollars paid by the pharmacist to the manufacturer).

P_c = the weighted average price of a new prescription for the relevant leading competitive drugs. Given the oligopolistic nature of the markets, the number of competitors examined was either three, four, or five, and these products accounted for the bulk of all the remaining turnover in the market not attributable to the NCE. The weights awarded are the relative sales figures of the competing products.

a. Important therapeutic gain: The drug may provide effective therapy or diagnosis (by virtue of greatly increased efficacy or safety) for a disease not adequately treated or diagnosed by any market drug, or it may provide markedly improved treatment of a disease through improved efficacy or safety (including decreased abuse potential).

b. Modest therapeutic gain: The drug has a modest but real advantage over other available marketed drugs. Advantages may be somewhat greater effectiveness, decreased adverse reactions, and less frequent dosing in situations where frequent dosage is a problem.

c. Little or no therapeutic gain: The drug essentially duplicates in medical importance and therapy one or more already existing drugs.

SOURCE: Reekie, "Price and Quality Competition in the United States Drug Industry," table 1.

Although evidence collected by Cocks and Virts and by Reekie suggests that prices of drugs are not immune to market forces, there is also evidence of significant price differentials between the original brand-name drugs and duplicate drugs of the same generic name.[18] Large drug firms argue that price differences between brand name and generic drugs are the result of differences in quality, and David Schwartzman presents evidence from a number of studies that generally confirm that brand-name drugs offer higher quality.[19]

Even if differences in quality between generic and brand-name drugs account for the entire difference between their prices, a similar argument cannot be made to explain the differences in price between drugs of a given generic name which are marketed under various brand names by major pharmaceutical firms. According to Charles T. Silloway, president of Ciba,

TABLE 25
EFFECTIVE WHOLESALE PRICES AND SALES REVENUE OF AMPICILLIN SOLD UNDER VARIOUS BRAND NAMES, 1973

Brand Name	Manufacturer	Year of Introduction	Price (250 mg/20 capsules) June 1973 (dollars)	Sale Revenue 1973 (thousands of dollars)
Pollycillin	Bristol	1963	2.66	23,086
SK-ampicillin	SmithKline	1971	2.25	3,326
Omnipen	Wyeth	1966	1.97	10,263
Amcill	Parke-Davis	1968	1.89	6,291
Penbritin	Ayerst	1964	1.84	6,170
Totacillin	Becchem USV	1969	1.73	2,630
Principen	Squibb	1967	1.65	11,809
Pen-A	Pfizer	1972	1.42	4,747

SOURCE: Schwartzman, *Innovation in the Pharmaceutical Industry*, tables 12.5 and 12.9.

reserpine produced by large firms met the U.S. Pharmacopoeia standards just as Serpasil, Ciba's brand, did.[20] Yet sales of Serpasil in 1973 amounted to more than than $3.8 million while the combined sales of Raused, Reserpoid, and Eskaserp, brand names of reserpine produced by Squibb, Upjohn, and SmithKline, respectively, amounted to only $104,000.[21]

Furthermore, even in the field of antibiotics, where Schwartzman says price competition is intense, there are significant price differences. As presented in table 25, ampicillin was sold by Bristol under the brand name Pollycillin for $2.66 (wholesale) per prescription in 1973, but the same prescription filled with Pen-A, the brand name of ampicillin by Pfizer, cost only $1.42, about half of Bristol's price. Yet sales of Pollycillin exceeded sales of Pen-A by a ratio of almost 5 to 1.

It seems that the cost of acquiring information on the quality and prices of drugs is sufficiently high that price differences can persist for a long time. The argument that increased availability of information can be expected to decrease price differentials is supported by John Cady's finding that prices of drugs are generally lower in states that allow pharmacists to advertise prices.[22]

Competition and Efficient Use of Resources

Although an average rate of return in excess of the normal rate of return can be interpreted as an indication of monopoly power or disequilibrium, an average rate of return at the normal rate of return does not necessarily imply the existence of perfect competition. When the average rate of return equals the normal rate of return, this may indicate the existence of monopolistic competition as described by Edward Chamberlin.[23] Monopolistic competition may exist when there is free entry if the cost function includes fixed costs. Product differentiation may lead to demand functions with less than perfect elasticity. In this case, entry of competitors with differentiated products will shift each demand function to a point where it is tangent to the average total cost function. At this point the economic profit is zero, or the average return is equal to the normal return.

It has been recognized that the existence of fixed costs, such as R & D costs, in the cost function may lead to situations in which marginal cost pricing will not lead to maximum economic welfare.[24] If fixed costs exist, marginal cost pricing may mean that these fixed costs cannot be retrieved by the producer through sales revenue, which may lead him to choose not to produce at all. As a consequence, the potential welfare surplus from this product will be totally lost. Michael Spence concludes that a second best solution is not easy to find, but that "[g]iven the profitability constraint under the market system, deviations from the marginal cost pricing are called for. Monopolistically competitive pricing may not be too far from the second best. In some special instances, it is the second best."[25]

It has been argued that much of the R & D activity of the pharmaceutical industry is of little value because the industry does not engage in much basic research and many of the innovative drugs are no more than "molecular manipulations" of existing drugs.[26] Comanor points out, however, that the industry's allocation of resources to development rather than to research is not necessarily inefficient from the standpoint of economic welfare.[27] According to Comanor, there exists a division of labor such that universities and other research institutions conduct basic research, and the pharmaceutical industry performs efficiently the task of transforming the results of that research into innovative drugs. In addition, the allocation of resources to molecular manipulation may not be inefficient. Larry Deutsch reported that drugs that were innovated through molecular manipulation yielded significant therapeutic gains. Eight out of eighteen drugs, reported by a panel of physicians to be the most significant, were the result of molecular manipulation.[28]

In terms of economic welfare, it is continuously debated whether advertising expenditures should be considered a waste of economic resources. The arguments and the evidence in this debate were reviewed by Yale Brozen and by H. Michael Mann and will not be repeated here.[29] The evidence does not clearly lead to the conclusion that advertising in general is wasteful.

In the pharmaceutical industry, the evidence suggests that advertising is used as a means of entry into the market rather than as a barrier to entry. In a cross-section study of a sample of seventeen therapeutic fields in the U.S. market, Telser found a positive relationship between the rate of entry into therapeutic fields and advertising intensity.[30] Telser's results are supported by evidence from a detailed case study by Ronald Bond and David Lean of the Federal Trade Commission.[31]

Bond and Lean focused on two therapeutic markets: antianginals, a market with no important patents and a large number of firms, and orally effective diuretics, a market in which patent protection allowed only a few firms to compete. They found that in both markets the leading firms "had promotion-to-sales ratios substantially lower than those of non-leading firms: the high market ratios reflected primarily the promotion of non-leading firms."[32] Advertising, it seems, was used as an avenue of entry for new entrants rather than as a barrier to entry by the leading firm. Bond and Lean concluded also that promotional efforts on behalf of drugs that offer no new therapeutic gain were not rewarded, but that "physicians can be persuaded to prescribe late-entering brands if those brands offer some therapeutic gain useful to a subset of patients."[33] Similar results were reported by Reekie, who found that a significant positive correlation existed between the rate of drug innovation and the intensity of advertising across therapeutic fields in the British pharmaceutical industry.[34]

Conclusion

The evidence generally supports the hypothesis that the pharmaceutical industry is competitive. The industry is characterized by continuous entry and market share instability, which are inconsistent with monopoly power.

The relative lack of price competition between original brand-name drugs and competitors following patent expiration can be explained by the existence of information costs. As information on the availability of substitute drugs and their prices becomes easier and less costly to acquire, price competition increases.

Notes

1. Joseph A. Califano, Jr., "What's Wrong with U.S. Health Care," *The Washington Post*, June 26, 1977.

2. Computed from U.S. Bureau of the Census, *1972 Census of Manufacturers*, Special Report Series, Concentration Ratios in Manufacturing, MC72(SR)-2, Washington, D.C., 1975, table 5.

3. H. M. Blake, "Legislative Proposals for Industrial Deconcentration," in *Industrial Concentration: The New Learning*, ed. H. J. Goldschmid et al. (Boston: Little, Brown and Company, 1974), pp. 340–60.

4. J. W. Markham, "Economic Incentives in the Drug Industry," in *Drugs in Our Society*, ed. P. Talalay (Baltimore: Johns Hopkins Press, 1964), p. 169; and L. G. Schifrin, "The Ethical Drug Industry: The Case for Compulsory Patent Licensing," *Antitrust Bulletin*, vol. 12 (Fall 1967), p. 901.

5. W. G. Shepherd, *Market Power and Economic Welfare* (New York: Random House, 1970), chap. 7.

6. D. L. Cocks and J. R. Virts, "Market Definition and Concentration in the Ethical Pharmaceutical Industry" (unpublished).

7. J. Bain, *Barriers to New Competition* (Cambridge, Mass.: Harvard University Press, 1956).

8. H. Demsetz, "Two Systems of Belief about Monopoly," in *Industrial Concentration: The New Learning*, ed. H. J. Goldschmidt et al. (Boston: Little, Brown and Company, 1974), p. 116.

9. W. S. Comanor, "Research and Competitive Product Differentiation in the Pharmaceutical Industry in the United States," *Economica*, vol. 31 (November 1964), pp. 372–84.

10. L. G. Telser, "The Supply Response to Shifting Demand in the Ethical Pharmaceutical Industry," in *Drug Development and Marketing*, ed. R. B. Helms (Washington, D.C.: American Enterprise Institute, 1975), pp. 207–23.

11. D. L. Cocks, "Product Innovation and the Dynamic Elements of Competition in the Ethical Pharmaceutical Industry," in *Drug Development and Marketing*, ed. R. B. Helms, pp. 225–54.

12. The firms are: Abbott, American Home Products, Bristol-Myers, Burroughs-Wellcome, Ciba-Geigy, Lederle, Lilly, Merck, Pfizer, Roche, Sandoz-Wander, Schering-Plough, Searle, SmithKline, Squibb, Upjohn, Warner-Lambert, and Winthrop.

13. G. C. Means, *Industrial Prices and Their Relative Inflexibility*, U.S. Congress, Senate, 74th Congress, 1st session, 1935, document 13; and "The Administered-Price Thesis Reconfirmed," *American Economic Review*, vol. 62 (June 1972), pp. 292–306.

14. Cited in J. W. Markham, "Economic Incentives in the Drug Industry," p. 171.

15. H. Steele, "Patent Restrictions and Price Competition in the Ethical Drug Industry," *Journal of Law and Economics*, vol. 12 (July 1964), pp. 198–203; P. M. Costello, "The Tetracycline Conspiracy: Structure Conduct and Performance in the Drug Industry," *Antitrust Law and Economics Review*, vol. 1 (Summer 1968), pp. 13–44.

16. D. L. Cocks and J. R. Virts, "Pricing Behavior of the Pharmaceutical Industry," *Journal of Business*, vol. 47 (July 1974), pp. 349–62.

17. W. D. Reekie, "Price and Quality Competition in the United States Drug Industry," *Journal of Industrial Economics*, vol. 26 (March 1978), pp. 223–37.

18. See, for example, Paul A. Brooke, *Resistant Prices* (New York: The Council on Economic Priorities, 1975).

19. D. Schwartzman, *Innovation in the Pharmaceutical Industry* (Baltimore: Johns Hopkins University Press, 1976), chap. 11.

20. Ibid., p. 244.

21. Ibid., p. 263, table 12-5.

22. J. F. Cady, *Restricted Advertising and Competition: The Case of Retail Drugs* (Washington, D.C.: American Enterprise Institute, 1976).

23. E. H. Chamberlin, *The Theory of Monopolistic Competition*, 8th ed., (Cambridge, Mass.: Harvard University Press, 1962).

24. K. J. Arrow, "Economic Welfare and the Allocation of Resources for Invention," in *The Rate and Direction of Invention Activity*, ed. R. R. Nelson, (Princeton, N.J.: Princeton University Press, 1962), pp. 609–26.

25. M. Spence, "Product Selection, Fixed Costs, and Monopolistic Competition," *Review of Economic Studies*, vol. 43 (June 1976), p. 234.

26. T. S. Lall, "The International Pharmaceutical Industry and Less Developed Countries, with Special Reference to India," *Bulletin of the Oxford Institute of Economics and Statistics*, vol. 36 (August 1974), pp. 143–72.

27. W. S. Comanor, "The Drug Industry and Medical Research: The Economics of the Kefauver Investigation," *Journal of Business*, vol. 39 (January 1969), pp. 12–18.

28. L. L. Deutsch, "Research Performance in the Ethical Drug Industry," *Marquette Business Review*, vol. 17 (Fall 1973), pp. 129–42.

29. Y. Brozen, "Entry Barriers: Advertising and Product Differentiation," in Goldschmid, *Industrial Concentration*, pp. 115–37; H. M. Mann, "Advertising, Concentration, and Profitability: The State of Knowledge, and Directions for Public Policy," in Goldschmid, *Industrial Concentration*, pp. 137–56.

30. L. G. Telser et al., "The Theory of Supply with Applications to the Ethical Pharmaceutical Industry," *Journal of Law and Economics*, vol. 18 (1975).

31. R. S. Bond and D. F. Lean, *Sales, Promotion and Product Differentiation in Two Prescription Drug Markets* (Washington, D.C.: Federal Trade Commission, February 1977).

32. Ibid., p. iv.

33. Ibid., p. 76.

34. W. D. Reekie, "Some Problems Associated with the Marketing of Ethical Pharmaceutical Products," *Journal of Industrial Economics*, vol. 19 (November 1970), pp. 33–49.

7
The Incentives for Drug Innovation

The decline in the return on drug innovation from 20.9 percent in 1954 to 10.3 percent in 1978 was the result of two major forces. The first was a gradual transformation of the pharmaceutical industry. The high returns in the early post–World War II period resulted from the great opportunities for drug innovation made possible by the discoveries that opened whole new research areas. As the industry undertook more R & D and more drugs became available, the competition among drugs decreased returns. The second major force contributing to the decline in the return on drug innovation was the increase in government regulation of pharmaceutical innovation. This raised the investment required to produce new drugs, with the consequence that the equilibrium output of innovation decreased.

The first part of this chapter discusses the effect of regulation on incentives to invest in R & D for drug innovation. The second part of the chapter discusses the effects on incentives to invest in R & D of the decreasing effective patent period and policies aimed at lowering drug prices.

Ethical Drug Regulation

Regulation of drugs is the responsibility of the Food and Drug Administration (FDA). No drug can be sold in the United States unless the FDA approves it, and the FDA approves only drugs that it finds safe and effective.

The authority of the FDA stems from the Food, Drug, and Cosmetic Act of 1938 and the 1962 amendments to that act. The 1938 act required that evidence be submitted to the FDA on the drug's safety as a condition for marketing it in the United States. It required the FDA to render a decision within sixty days after the submission of an application for permission to market a new drug. The 1962 amendments to the act required that drug firms provide evidence on the drug's efficacy, in addition to the evidence on safety. The 1962 amendments also introduced controls on the clinical stages of the drug development process and restrictions on claims that can be made by manufacturers in advertising drugs. Although proof of safety was a requirement of the 1938 act, there is evidence that reviews of safety after 1962 have become more stringent.[1]

Although it is agreed that drugs should be safe and effective, the FDA's approach to these goals caused a number of undesirable side-effects on the incentives for drug innovation. The FDA admits that some conflict exists. According to J. Richard Crout, director of the Bureau of Drugs of the FDA:

> The issue isn't whether regulation cuts down on innovation. Indeed it does. There's hardly any way that regulation can stimulate innovation. Those are cross purposes. The issue is whether the regulation accomplishes some higher purpose and does so with a minimum inhibition of research. That's hard. I won't say it's easy.[2]

The discussion of the benefits and costs of drug regulation has focused primarily on the effects of the 1962 amendments to the 1938 act. James M. Jondrow estimates that the value of benefits of the 1962 amendments to consumers exceeded its costs by a ratio of 2.24.[3] Jondrow assumed, however, that no part of the decline in drug innovation after 1962 was due to the 1962 regulations, which obviously results in an underestimation of the cost to consumers of these regulations. Sam Peltzman estimated the reduction in the flow of new drugs attributable to the 1962 regulation and the amount of the consequent loss of benefits.[4] By his estimates, there was an annual welfare loss of $350–450 million because a smaller number of new drugs appeared on the market each year. The welfare gain due to decreased use of ineffective drugs was less than $100 million, resulting in a net welfare loss of several hundred million dollars each year.

Grabowski, Vernon, and Thomas compared the use of new drugs in the United States and Britain and rejected the hypothesis that the 1962 regulations are not responsible for the decline in drug innovation in the United States in the post-1962 period.[5] William Wardell and Louis Lasagna found that a "drug lag" exists between the United States and Britain. New drugs are generally available earlier in Britain than in the United States.

> The protection conferred by delaying the introduction of new drugs needs to be weighed against the therapeutic losses thus incurred. From the present evidence, it appears that each country has gained in some ways and lost in others. On balance, however, it is difficult to argue that the United States has escaped an inordinate amount of new drug toxicity by its conservative approach; it has gained little else. On the other hand, it is relatively easy to show that Britain has gained by having effective drugs available sooner. Furthermore, the costs of this policy in terms of damage due to adverse drug reactions have been small compared with the existing levels of damage produced by older drugs. There appear to be no other therapeutic costs of any consequence in Britain. In view of the clear benefits demonstrable from some of the drugs introduced into Britain, it appears that the United States has lost more than it has gained from adopting a more conservative approach than did Britain in the post-thalidomide era.[6]

TABLE 26

R & D Expenditures of the U.S.
Ethical Pharmaceutical Industry, 1952–1977

Year	Total R & D Expenditures, Current Dollars[a] (millions)	Total R & D Expenditures, Constant Dollars[b] (millions)	Annual Real Rate of Growth of R & D Expenditures (percent)	Ratio of R & D Performed Abroad by U.S. Firms to R & D Performed Domestically (percent)
1952	59.9	103.3		n.a.
			12.4	
1957	120.7	185.6		n.a.
			12.7	
1962	238.0	337.3		5.8
			9.1	
1967	412.4	521.9		9.2
			5.0	
1972	666.8	666.8		11.0
			4.6	
1977	1,181.8	834.0		20.0

n.a. = not available.
   a. For human use (veterinary use pharmaceutical R & D is excluded).
   b. Deflated by GNP price deflator (1972 = 100).
Source: Pharmaceutical Manufacturers Association, *Annual Survey Report*, Washington, D.C., various issues.

Compliance with FDA regulations as administered by FDA reviewing officers added considerably to the cost of drug innovations after 1962. It is difficult to determine what proportion of R & D costs are due to regulation, but Grabowski, Vernon, and Thomas estimated that the 1962 amendments have, at a minimum, doubled the R & D investment required for a new drug.[7] To estimate the effect of the regulatory costs added by the 1962 change on the return on drug innovation, the expected return on the 1978 drugs was reestimated under the assumption that R & D figures were half the actual figures. Removal of the added regulatory costs resulted in an increase in return from 10.3 percent to 13.6 percent, assuming that the increase in the delays since 1962 caused by the new regulatory regime remains unchanged.

The effect of regulatory costs is significant. It is especially so since the 10.3 percent figure is below the cost of capital. Returns below the cost of capital can be expected to lead to the decline of investment in pharmaceutical R & D relative to what it otherwise might be. Signs of this trend are already evident. The rate of growth of R & D expenditure for human use drugs was much lower in the 1960s than in the 1950s, and the declining trend is continuing. In addition, as shown in table 26, U.S. firms are performing an increasing proportion of their R & D in other countries, eroding the position of the United States as a leader in drug innovation.

A number of alternatives have been suggested to counter the trend of decreasing incentives for pharmaceutical R & D caused by FDA regulations. The more modest of these alternatives involve increasing the efficiency of the regulatory process, thereby reducing some of the regulatory costs. More radical alternatives involve the abandonment of the requirement for FDA approval of drugs in favor of a new role for the FDA as a provider of information on drugs. Since consumers can sue for damages the manufacturers of drugs that are not safe or effective, there may be sufficient incentives for drug firms to introduce only safe and effective drugs even without FDA regulations.[8]

If the profitability of drug innovation in the early post–World War II period made it possible to impose costly regulations on drug innovation, the low and declining return of recent years suggests that decisions on the desirable level of regulation must take into consideration their effect on R & D costs and incentives for innovation.

Patents, Trademarks, and Generic Substitution

Increased regulation of drug innovation not only resulted in increased R & D costs per drug, but also lengthened the time required for the development of drugs. A consequence of this trend is a continuous erosion of the protection afforded to innovators of drugs by the patent system.

The patent system is designed to enable those who invest to capture a portion of the economic return from their investment. The patent statute, enacted in 1836, provides for a seventeen-year period during which "an inventor has the right to exclude all others from making, using, or selling his invention within the United States, its territories and possessions." Thus, the patent statute establishes a monopoly for the investor that is protected by law. Such monopoly rights are deemed necessary since appropriation by the inventor of information contained in an invention is difficult. It is much less costly to copy an invention than to produce one. In the absence of patent protection, we may expect investment for invention by private firms to be less than socially optimal.[9]

An invention is not protected by the patent statute until a patent is issued. Still, the act of marking the product "patent pending" will usually deter copying it during the time that elapses between the date of filing for a patent with the U.S. Patent Office and the patent grant date. The nominal period of patent protection is always longer than seventeen years because some time is necessary for evaluation of the patent application by the U.S. Patent Office. The protection provided to an inventor by the patent statute, however, does not become effective until he can exploit it in the marketplace. We may define the "effective period" of a patent as the period starting with the market introduction of a product using the invention and ending with the patent expiration date.

Although there are several types of patents that apply to drugs, most drug patents can be described as product patents because they claim as an invention the composition of the matter constituting the drug.[10] A drug is invented when a chemical compound is synthesized and found to have some therapeutic utility. As a practical matter, a drug firm must apply for a patent at this point. Any delay may result in a loss of the rights for a patent because a competitor may be the first to file for a patent.[11]

The invention of a drug, however, is only one step in the process that may eventually lead to commercial marketing. A chemical entity with indications of therapeutic utility must undergo a lengthy development process and be approved by the Food and Drug Administration before it can appear on the market and enjoy the fruits of the protection provided by the relevant patent. The seventeen-year period provided by the patent statute has not changed since the patent statute was enacted. The effective period of protection for drug patents, however, has changed considerably. Using a sample of 126 drugs (new single-chemical entities) introduced into the U.S. market during the 1949–1975 period, it was possible to estimate the effective period of drug patents as follows:[12]

$$EP = 38.9744 - 0.374672 \, IN \qquad R^2 = 0.3175$$
$$(12.4974) \; (-7.59413)$$

where EP = the effective period of a drug patent (years) and IN = U.S. market introduction year (indicated by the last two digits). The predicted effective period of patents for drugs introduced during 1950–1978 is presented in table 27. Note that there was a continuous decline in the effective period of drug patents during the time span under study. These results are in general agreement with Schwartzman's estimate of an average of 13.1 years of effective period for drugs introduced during 1966–1973.[13] They are also consistent with a study by the Center for Study of Drug Development, University of Rochester, which found an estimated decline from 13.8 years in 1966 to 8.9 years in 1977 in the effective life of drug patents.[14]

The decline in the effective patent period is significant, however, only if the expiration of a drug patent opens the way to considerable entry or price reduction. The evidence on the long life cycle of original drugs, presented in chapter 4, suggests, however, that innovators of drugs are usually successful in maintaining the market position of drugs long after their patents expired. The trademark law plays a major role in maintaining this market position. A trademark is defined as "a name, symbol, or other device identifying a product, officially registered and legally restricted to the use of

TABLE 27
Average Effective Period of Patents
for Drugs Introduced in 1950–1978

Year of U.S. Market Introduction	Effective Period of Patent Protection (years) Prediction Based on the Equation for EP[a]
1950	20.2
1951	19.9
1952	19.5
1953	19.1
1954	18.7
1955	18.4
1956	18.0
1957	17.6
1958	17.2
1959	16.9
1960	16.5
1961	16.1
1962	15.7
1963	15.4
1964	15.0
1965	14.6
1966	14.2
1967	13.9
1968	13.5
1969	13.1
1970	12.7
1971	12.4
1972	12.0
1973	11.6
1974	11.2
1975	10.9
1976	10.5
1977	10.1
1978	9.7

a. The equation for EP (the effective period of a drug patent) appears in the text.

the owner or manufacturer."[15] For example, a manufacturer who wishes to market an analgesic bearing the generic name acetaminophen may do so as there is no patent in effect to prohibit it. A manufacturer may market the drug under the generic name, or he may create a name for it that can be registered as a trademark. He does not have the option of naming it Tylenol, however, which is a registered trademark of acetaminophen made by McNeil, or any of the trademarks that are already registered to other manufacturers of acetaminophen. Unlike patents, which have a limited period during which they are in effect, trademarks can be renewed indefinitely as long as they are in use in interstate commerce.

Until quite recently almost all states had laws prohibiting the substitution of a generic drug or a different brand for the brand prescribed by the physician—but this situation changed rapidly during the past few years. As of December 1979, forty-four states and the District of Columbia have repealed antisubstitution laws and now allow substitution unless prohibited by the prescribing physician.[16] The goal of the change in policy was to save money for customers by allowing them to shop for the lowest-priced drug of a given generic name. This goal is shared by the Maximum Allowable Cost (MAC) program, mandating drug substitution in government health programs.

As is the case with FDA regulations on drug innovation, there is a trade-off between low prices of drugs to consumers and incentives for innovation of drugs. Comanor described the problem in the following way:

> The issue of public policy with regard to the drug industry is concerned precisely with the existence of a trade-off between high levels of research and high prices at one end of the spectrum and low research and prices at the other. If patents, trademarks and advertising were not permitted, I think most of us would agree that drug prices would be much lower. At the same time, little research would be carried on. And if we had a patent system which permitted a hundred-year restriction on competition rather than the current figure of 17 years, more research would probably be carried on. At the same time, prices would be even higher than they are currently. The interesting question then is what combination of research and prices is optimal given that neither extreme is optimal?[17]

It is too early to assess the effect of the recent changes in the law allowing generic substitution, especially since the Federal Trade Commission (FTC) is attempting to change the laws further to facilitate generic substitution.[18] Nonetheless, we can assess the potential effect of generic substitution on the return on drug innovation under the assumption that the FTC effort is successful.[19]

The expected rate of return on drugs introduced in 1978 was reestimated assuming a patent period of ten years[20] and assuming that prices of drugs drop after patent expiration to a level equal to production costs including return on capital services but no return on R & D (or that sales equal zero). Under these conditions the return declines to 6.6 percent from 10.3 percent. Thus, it seems possible that the attempt to save money for consumers through lower prices of drugs might result in further reduction of incentives to innovate drugs.

Pending legislation, which recognizes the effect of regulation on the effective patent period, aims to extend the patent period to compensate for the loss of the development time of drugs.

A Look to the Future

The story of the pharmaceutical industry exemplifies the extraordinary vitality of a market economy. Opportunities for drug innovation, opened up by scientific discovery, were seized by entrepreneurs. These opportunities resulted in new drugs that enable people to lead longer and healthier lives. The opportunities also resulted in high profits to the enterprising firms and the profits encouraged more innovation.

The declining rate of return on drug innovation does not necessarily mean that the industry is declining. Many diseases still await cure, and new research avenues, such as genetic engineering, show promise. A steady stream of important new drugs continues to flow, and we may still witness scientific breakthroughs and flurries of drug innovation exceeding those of the past.

It is not likely, however, that we will see industry-wide average returns on drug innovation that are double the cost of capital, as was the case in the 1950s and early 1960s. The pharmaceutical industry today is mature. Many well-established pharmaceutical companies exist with expertise in drug innovation. Companies that find new and profitable research avenues will find that other companies are quite capable of taking the same avenues. The resulting competition is likely to keep returns on drug innovation close to the cost of capital.

Notes

1. H. Grabowski, *Drug Regulation and Innovation* (Washington, D.C.: American Enterprise Institute, 1976), p. 15.

2. J. R. Crout, Transcript of Statement to the HEW Review Panel on New Drug Regulation, *FDC Reports*, April 26, 1976.

3. J. M. Jondrow, "A Measure of the Monetary Benefits and Costs to Consumers of the Regulation of Prescription Drug Effectiveness" (Ph.D. dissertation, University of Wisconsin, 1972).

4. S. Peltzman, *Regulation of Pharmaceutical Innovation* (Washington, D.C.: American Enterprise Institute, 1974).

5. H. G. Grabowski, J. M. Vernon, and L. G. Thomas, "Estimating the Effects of Regulation on Innovation: An International Comparative Analysis of the Pharmaceutical Industry," *Journal of Law and Economics*, vol. 21 (April 1978) p. 133–63.

6. W. M. Wardell and L. Lasagna, *Regulation and Drug Development* (Washington, D.C.: American Enterprise Institute, 1975), p. 105.

7. Grabowski, Vernon, and Thomas, "Estimating the Effects of Regulation on Innovation," p. 159.

8. See the discussion by G. Calabresi, "Comments on Preclinical Problems of New Drug Development," in *Regulating New Drugs*, ed. R. L. Landau (Chicago: University of Chicago Press, 1973), pp. 54–60.

9. A comprehensive discussion is provided in K. J. Arrow, "Economic Welfare and the Allocation of Resources for Invention," in *The Rate and Direction of Inventive Activity*, ed. R. Nelson (Princeton, N.J.: Princeton University Press, 1962). Arrow argues that the patent system provides less than socially optimal incentives for allocating resources to invention since not all information contained in an invention can be appropriated even with the aid of a patent.

10. E. W. Kitch, "The Patent System and the New Drug Application," in *Regulating New Drugs*, ed. R. L. Landau (Chicago: University of Chicago Press, 1973), p. 82–107.

11. Ibid.

12. The sample was compiled from data published in Frost & Sullivan, Inc., *The Generic Drug Market* (New York, 1972), and a list of drugs selected randomly by Louis Leaman Company, a consulting firm.

13. D. Schwartzman, *Innovation in the Pharmaceutical Industry* (Baltimore: The Johns Hopkins University Press, 1976), chap. 8.

14. Unpublished report, 1979.

15. William Morris, ed., *American Heritage Dictionary of the English Language* (Boston: Houghton Mifflin, 1971).

16. Compiled by the Pharmaceutical Manufacturers Association.

17. W. Comanor, in *The Economics of Drug Innovation*, ed. J. D. Cooper (Washington, D.C.: The American University, 1970), p. 225.

18. Federal Trade Commission, *Drug Product Selection* (Washington, D.C.: FTC, 1979).

19. Preliminary evidence in Meir Statman's "The Effect of Patent Expiration on the Market Position of Drugs," *Managerial and Decision Economics*, vol. 2, no. 2 (1981), pp. 61–66, reprinted in R. B. Helms, ed., *Drugs and Health, Economic Issues and Policy Objectives* (Washington, D.C.: American Enterprise Institute 1981), pp. 140–51, shows that original drugs suffered very little loss of market share following patent expiration. This may be due to the slow adjustment to the changes in the law or to a more permanent resistance to substitution on the part of physicians, pharmacists, and consumers.

20. This is approximately the effective patent period for drugs introduced in 1978. See table 27.

Appendix A
Estimates of the Life Cycle of Drugs in the Domestic Market

Analysis of the life cycle of drugs is based upon data on annual sales revenue during 1967–1975 of NCE drugs introduced during 1940–1974, and data on annual sales revenue during 1972–1975 of combination drugs introduced during 1954–1974.[1] The introduction stage of the life cycle was estimated as the first nine years, and the annual rates of growth of sales revenue of the average NCE drug during the introduction stage are presented in table 28.

The rate of growth was computed as the compounded annual rate of growth of sales revenue of the average NCE drug during the second to ninth years of each drug group. (A drug group includes all NCE drugs introduced by PMA members during a given year.) Sales during the first year were excluded because they depend upon when a drug was introduced during the year. Since sales revenue data were available on computer tape only for nine consecutive years, 1967–1975, the rate of growth is based upon the time span within the introduction stage for which data were available. Pre-1963 and post-1971 drug groups were excluded from the computation of the rate of growth during the introduction stage because the relevant available data were considered too limited to be reliable.

The annual rates of growth of sales revenue of the average NCE drug during the plateau stage (from the tenth year and on) were computed in a similar fashion and are presented in table 29. The use of a section of the life cycle to estimate the entire life cycle may be subject to bias if there are major fluctuations in the sales revenue of the average drug during its life cycle, other than the movement through the introduction stage and into the plateau stage. To examine the likelihood of such bias, sales revenue data of NCE and combination drugs introduced during 1957 and 1962 were analyzed for the period starting with the year of introduction and continuing through 1975.[2] The life cycle pattern of the average drug in these samples supports the view that no significant volatility exists in the life cycle of the *average* drug. The hypothesis of a smooth life cycle pattern is

TABLE 28
GROWTH OF SALES REVENUE OF AN AVERAGE NCE DRUG DURING THE INTRODUCTION STAGE, FOR DRUGS INTRODUCED EACH YEAR, 1963–1971

Year of U.S. Market Introduction	Annual Rate of Growth of Sales Revenue (percent)	Period during Which the Rate of Growth Was Computed
1963	22.5	1967–1971
1964	17.7	1967–1972
1965	−1.0	1967–1973
1966	23.8	1967–1974
1967	15.1	1968–1975
1968	7.4	1969–1975
1969	10.6	1970–1975
1970	8.0	1971–1975
1971	17.5	1972–1975
Average annual rate of growth	13.5	

NOTE: The introduction stage is the first nine years of a drug after market introduction. Estimates of growth are based on sales during the second to ninth years.
SOURCE: IMS America, Ltd., *U.S. Pharmaceutical Market, Drug Stores and Hospitals* (Ambler, Pa., various years).

also supported by the shape of the 1967–1975 segment of the life cycles, for which complete data were available.

Another bias may arise if the rate of growth during 1967–1975 was different from the average rate of growth during a longer period. Indeed, we find that although the annual rate of growth of the ethical drug market, measured in terms of revenue, during 1967–1975 was 10 percent, it was only 8 percent during the longer period 1950–1975.[3] The more rapid growth for the later part of this period may have been the result of the introduction of the Medicare and Medicaid programs, as well as more rapid price increases. To correct for the bias introduced by the difference in the rates of growth, 2 percent was subtracted from the average annual rates of growth presented in tables 28 and 29. The estimate of the annual rate of growth of sales revenue during the introduction stage is, therefore, 11.5 percent. Since the unadjusted estimated annual rate of growth during the plateau stage, 2.4 percent, is insignificantly different from the adjustment of 2 percent, it was assumed that there was no growth during the plateau stage.

The analysis of the life cycle of the average NCE drug is based on sales revenue during 1967–1975 of drugs introduced since 1940. Since no decline

TABLE 29

GROWTH OF SALES REVENUE OF AN AVERAGE NCE DRUG DURING THE PLATEAU STAGE, FOR DRUGS INTRODUCED EACH YEAR, 1940–1962

Year of U.S. Market Introduction	Annual Rate of Growth (percent)	Period during Which the Rate of Growth Was Computed
1940	8.0	1967–1975
1941	3.2	1967–1975
1942	8.0	1967–1975
1943	−7.7	1967–1975
1944	−0.9	1967–1975
1945	3.6	1967–1975
1946	6.4	1967–1975
1947	−3.0	1967–1975
1948	0.1	1967–1975
1949	−2.1	1967–1975
1950	2.2	1967–1975
1951	10.8	1967–1975
1952	2.9	1967–1975
1953	−5.3	1967–1975
1954	0.0	1967–1975
1955	5.0	1967–1975
1956	0.8	1967–1975
1957	2.2	1967–1975
1958	3.9	1967–1975
1959	6.6	1968–1975
1960	1.2	1969–1975
1961	9.0	1970–1975
1962	−0.4	1971–1975
Average annual rate of growth	2.4	

NOTE: The plateau stage begins with the tenth year after market introduction.
SOURCE: IMS America, Ltd., *U.S. Pharmaceutical Market, Drug Stores and Hospitals* (Ambler, Pa., various years).

was observed in the data, the length of the life cycle was estimated to be at least thirty-five years.

Data on sales revenue of combination drugs were collected for a four-year period, 1972–1975. Estimates of the rates of growth of sales revenue of combination drugs are less reliable than the rates of growth computed for NCE drugs, which were based upon a nine-year period. In addition, data for combination drugs were collected only for drugs introduced since 1954,

TABLE 30
GROWTH OF SALES REVENUE DURING 1972–1975
OF AN AVERAGE COMBINATION DRUG, FOR DRUGS
INTRODUCED EACH YEAR DURING 1954–1971

Year of U.S. Market Introduction	Annual Rate of Growth of Sales (percent)	Number of Drugs in the Sample
1954	−3.3	18
1955	9.0	18
1956	11.6	18
1957	−15.3	34
1958	1.8	18
1959	8.3	18
1960	9.5	18
1961	23.0	18
1962	1.9	31
1963	−4.2	18
1964	4.9	18
1965	16.8	18
1966	11.1	18
1967	13.9	18
1968	14.9	18
1969	3.5	18
1970	19.9	18
1971	10.2	15

SOURCE: IMS America, Ltd., *U.S. Pharmaceutical Market, Drug Stores and Hospitals* (Ambler, Pa., various years).

since no annual lists of combination drugs were available for earlier periods. The annual rate of growth of the average combination drugs introduced during 1954–1971 is presented in table 30.

The narrow scope of the data on combination drugs does not allow a detailed analysis of their life cycle, but there is no suggestion in the available data that the life cycle of the average combination drug differs from that of NCE drugs. Therefore, it was assumed that the life cycle of NCE drugs applies to combination drugs too.

So far, we have estimated the general pattern of the life cycle of the average drug. The life cycle of the average drug is composed of a nine-year introduction stage, during which sales revenue increases at an annual rate of 11.5 percent. This is followed by a period during which growth levels off. The total length of the life cycle is at least thirty-five years. We can now turn to the estimation of the level of sales revenue of average drugs introduced during the period 1954–1978. Table 31 presents the sales revenue of the

TABLE 31
Sales Revenue of an Average Drug, for Drugs Introduced Each Year by PMA Member Firms, 1952–1978

Year of U.S. Introduction	Average NCE Drug ($000) (1)	Average Combination Drug ($000) (2)	Ratio of No. of Combination Drugs to NCE Drugs (3)	Average Drug Unit ($000) (1) + [(2) × (3)]
1952	1,461	n.a.	6.27	2,388
1953	658	n.a.	4.18	1,267
1954	2,110	148	5.53	2,928
1955	1,777	575	6.85	5,714
1956	1,513	522	4.72	3,976
1957	1,697	127	4.07	2,214
1958	4,057	659	4.30	6,889
1959	3,734	1,011	2.43	6,187
1960	3,168	2,173	3.49	10,748
1961	2,495	2,661	2.87	10,128
1962	1,106	568	4.15	3,375
1963	23,274	123	6.29	24,048
1964	5,472	557	6.27	8,963
1965	4,520	4,566	2.91	17,821
1966	17,347	2,245	3.91	26,123
1967	6,455	2,190	1.30	9,311
1968	3,963	2,915	4.27	16,418
1969	3,465	757	3.00	5,736
1970	3,565	1,265	2.13	6,253
1971	7,218	1,114	1.64	9,048
1972	3,095	350	1.40	3,585
1973	3,633	811	0.76	4,253
1974	6,555	3,247	0.88	9,396
1975	3,850	2,852	1.73	8,793
1976	8,741	1,827	0.86	10,307
1977	7,398	778	1.10	8,254
1978	6,913	3,287	0.58	8,816

NOTE: 1975 sales revenue are reported for drugs introduced during 1952–1974; 1978 sales revenue are reported for drugs introduced during 1975–1977. Sales revenue in 1979 for drugs introduced in 1978 were estimated as two times sales revenue during the first six months of 1979. Data on the number of combination drugs introduced in 1952 and 1953 or their revenue were not available. Data for 1954 were used as estimates. A drug unit is defined as one NCE plus a proportion of combination drugs equal to the ratio of combination drugs to the NCE drugs introduced in a given year.
n.a. = not available.
SOURCE: IMS America, Ltd., *U.S. Pharmaceutical Market, Drug Stores and Hospitals* (Ambler, Pa., various years).

average drug unit introduced during 1952–1978.

The entire life cycle of a drug unit can now be estimated by applying the parameters of the life cycle, discussed previously, to the sales revenue of an average drug unit. The estimated domestic sales revenue of an average drug unit at the end of the introduction stage (ninth year) of the life cycle is presented in table 6.[4]

Notes

1. The data include all NCE drugs introduced into the U.S. market during 1940–1949, all NCE drugs introduced into the U.S. market by PMA members during 1950–1974, and samples of combination drugs introduced by members of the PMA into the U.S. market during 1954–1974. Sales revenue data relate to specific brand names and are aggregated over all dosage forms and potencies. The source of sales revenue data is IMS America, Ltd., *U.S. Pharmaceutical Market, Drug Stores and Hospitals*, Ambler, Pa. These data were made available to me on tape by Pfizer, Inc. (Data on pre-1967 sales revenue were not available on tape.) Data on new drug introductions are from Paul deHaen, Inc., *New Drug Survey*, New York (various issues). Annual lists of PMA members were made available to me by the PMA.

2. The samples included thirty-two NCE drugs and thirty-four combination drugs introduced by PMA members in 1957, and eighteen NCE drugs and thirty-one combination drugs introduced by PMA members in 1962.

3. U.S. sales of human dosage ethical drugs by drug firms were $1,013 million in 1950, $3,226 million in 1967, and $6,895 million in 1975 (data from PMA, *Annual Survey Report*, various issues).

4. IMS data on sales in the U.S. market exclude parts of the domestic markets. Specifically, the data do not include sales to the federal government and its hospitals and sales to clinics and practitioners (IMS America, Ltd., *U.S. Pharmaceutical Market, Drug Stores and Hospitals*). The PMA reported that 1975 domestic sales of ethical drugs amounted to $6,690 million free on board. IMS reported that sales to drugstores and hospitals included in its audit amounted to $6,085 million, which is 91 percent of the total domestic ethical drug market as reported by the PMA. IMS figures were multiplied by 1/0.91 to obtain the estimates presented in table 6.

Appendix B

The Number of Drugs Introduced Annually, the R & D Period, and the Distribution of R & D Expenditures over the R & D Period

Table 8 presents the number of NCE and combination drugs introduced annually by members of the PMA and the annual R & D expenditures by members of the PMA.

The R & D Period

The research stage of the R & D process of a drug is completed when a discovery is made of a new chemical entity that exhibits some desirable biological activity, without obvious excess toxicity. The research stage includes: (1) synthesis and extraction of single chemical entities, (2) biological screening and pharmacological testing of these chemical entities, and (3) first toxicity tests.[1]

According to Earle Arnow, these research steps last about one year.[2] The estimate of a one-year research period is, however, subject to a qualification. In some cases, preliminary work is carried out to determine which chemicals should be sought and subjected to tests. Such work may be based on research by the pharmaceutical firm or by outside organizations that make their findings available to the medical research community. In these cases, the research stage may last for more than one year. Such preliminary work, however, which may be called basic research, does not constitute a significant portion of the total research and development expenditures of the pharmaceutical firms.[3]

The development stage of a drug starts when the research stage is completed, and ends with the market introduction of the drug. Estimates of the development period point to a general increase in the development period over time. Using a sample of NCE drugs introduced in the 1950s and early 1960s, Jerome Schnee estimated the development period to be two years.[4] Clymer, in a 1970 study, estimated the prevailing development period to be five to seven years.[5] Louis H. Sarett estimated that the development period, excluding FDA approval, increased from 2 years in 1958–1962 to 4 years in 1963–1967, and from 5.5 to 7 years in 1968–1972.[6]

The following section describes the estimation of the changes in the development period of NCE drugs introduced during 1951–1978, which are presented in table 9.

It was assumed that the beginning of the development stage of an NCE drug generally coincides with the filing for a patent on that drug.[7] Using a sample of 126 NCE drugs introduced during 1949–1975, the following equation was estimated:

$$D = -16.7783 + 0.353099\ I \qquad R^2 = 0.3878$$
$$(-6.66196) \quad (8.86197)$$

where D = the development period for a drug (in years) and I = year of U.S. market introduction (the year is indicated by the last two digits). This equation indicates that the development period increased by a third of a year with the passage of each year during this period.

The Distribution of R & D Expenditures over the R & D Period

The R & D process of a drug may be described as a series of tests that a chemical entity has to pass. Each test may lead to a successive test if the result of the test is positive, or to the abandonment of that chemical entity if the result is negative. The final outcome of this process may be either a marketable drug or a chemical entity that is abandoned at some stage of the R & D process.

The probability that a chemical entity will move successfully from a given test to the next test may be called survivor probability. If such probabilities are known, and if we also know the cost per chemical entity of performing each test, or stage in the R & D process, then it is possible to calculate the expected distribution of R & D expenditures over time that are associated with one drug that has successfully completed the entire R & D process. Such cost estimates for the successful drug will also include the expenditures for work on chemical entities that did not successfully complete the entire R & D process.

For estimation purposes the research stage was separated from the development stage. This is because the survivor probability in the research stage is particularly low. As noted previously, the research stage lasts one year and includes synthesis and extraction of chemical entities, biological screening and pharmacological testing, and first toxicity tests. Table 32 presents a breakdown of R & D expenditures of PMA members, by function, in 1975. Synthesis, extraction, biological screening, and pharmacological testing account for approximately 39 percent of the total R & D expenditures. The share of toxicity and safety testing is approximately 10

TABLE 32

DISTRIBUTION OF THE DOMESTIC R & D EXPENDITURES
OF PMA MEMBER FIRMS, BY FUNCTION, 1975

Function	Percent of Total
Synthesis, extraction, biological screening, pharmacological testing	39
Toxicology and safety testing	10
Clinical evaluation	25
Dosage formulation, stability, testing, bio-availability studies, and process development	23
Regulatory expenses	3
	100

NOTE: Expenses marked "other" were excluded.
SOURCE: PMA, *Annual Survey Report, 1975–1976*, table 28.

percent. Only one-third of this expenditure, however, can be attributed to the research stage.[8] Thus, the total share of research expenditures amounts to approximately 42.5 percent of the total R & D expenditures.

Since the figures in table 32 represent a breakdown of annual expenditures, and since the research stage lasts one year, we can conclude that the research expenditures associated with one drug that reached the completion of the R & D process amount to 42.5 percent of the total R & D expenditures of such a drug. This estimate of the share of research expenditures is not very different from Schwartzman's estimate of a 50 percent research share, which was based upon inquiries to manufacturers.[9]

Stauffer postulates, on the basis of certain assumptions on the survivor probabilities and the distribution of R & D expenditures over the R & D period of a drug that reaches the point of completion, that the distribution over time of R & D expenditures associated with one completed drug is triangular, with a peak at the beginning of the period.[10] Simulation with a model of R & D expenditures, using actual data on survivor probabilities and R & D expenditures, also resulted in a triangular distribution of development expenditures over the development period of a drug that reached completion.[11] This distribution is presented in figure 5.

Notes

1. A comprehensive description of the R & D process of drugs can be found in L. E. Arnow, *Health in a Bottle* (Philadelphia: J. B. Lippincott Co., 1970).

2. Ibid., p. 41.

3. Stanford Research Institute, *The United States Health Products to 1980* (Menlo Park, Calif.: Stanford Research Institute, 1973).

4. E. Mansfield et al., *Research and Innovation in the Modern Corporation* (New York: W. W. Norton & Co., Inc., 1971), pp. 65–67.

5. H. A. Clymer, "The Changing Costs and Risks of Pharmaceutical Innovation," in *The Economics of Drug Innovation,* ed. J. D. Cooper (Washington, D.C.: The American University, 1970), pp. 109–24.

6. L. H. Sarett, "FDA Regulations and Their Influence on Future R & D," *Research Management,* vol. 17 (March 1975), pp. 18–20.

7. E. W. Kitch, "The Patent System and the New Drug Application," in *Regulating New Drugs,* ed. R. L. Landau (Chicago: The University of Chicago Center for Policy Studies, 1973), pp. 82–107.

8. Arnow divided toxicity tests into First Toxicity Tests, which lasted for three months and were included in the research stage, and Subacute Toxicity Tests, which lasted for six months and were considered as part of the development stage. The total expenditures for toxicity and safety tests were divided according to the proportion of the time required for them (Arnow, *Health in a Bottle,* p. 41).

9. D. Schwartzman, "Pharmaceutical R & D Expenditures and Rates of Return," in *Drug Development and Marketing,* ed. R. B. Helms (Washington, D.C.: American Enterprise Institute, 1975), p. 66.

10. T. R. Stauffer, "Profitability Measures in the Pharmaceutical Industry," in Helms, *Drug Development and Marketing,* p. 106.

11. A. D. Bender et al., "Simulation of R & D Investment Strategies," *Omega,* vol. 4 (February 1976), pp. 67–77. I am indebted to Dr. A. D. Bender and E. B. Pyle III, of Smith, Kline and French Laboratories for performing the simulation for me.

Appendix C
The Outlook for the U.S. Ethical Pharmaceutical Industry in Foreign Markets

According to table 7, which shows the ratio of global to domestic sales revenue of the U.S. pharmaceutical industry, the rate of growth of foreign sales of ethical drugs exceeded the rate of growth of domestic sales. The estimates in table 7 are based on data for the period 1954–1977. In the future, foreign markets may follow a different path from that suggested by a simple extrapolation of the trend in the past.

Table 33 provides a breakdown of the worldwide ethical-drug market and the U.S. share of it. The U.S. market was clearly the largest single market in 1975, but it made up only 17 percent of the global market. More significantly, the market share held by U.S. firms in major foreign ethical-drug markets was small. These figures seem to indicate that the U.S. pharmaceutical industry may not have yet exhausted the potential to expand in foreign markets.

Several problems exist, however, on the route to continued expansion. In the West German market, firms such as Hoechst-Roussel and Boehringer-Ingleheim offer formidable competition to American firms. In France, there is strong sentiment against multinationals, in addition to a restrictive attitude toward the pharmaceutical industry. The Italian market presents problems of rapid inflation and political instability. The U.S. penetration into the British market is already significant, and opportunities for further expansion are limited. The large Japanese market, however, still offers much growth potential for U.S. firms.

The problems of individual markets and the general emphasis in many countries on the problems of rising medical costs may mean that the period of rapid expansion of the foreign market in ethical drugs is over. Thus, the rate of return on drugs was estimated based on the alternative assumptions that the ratio of global to domestic sales of ethical drugs would stabilize at the projected 1980 level, and the projected 1990 level.

TABLE 33

SALES REVENUE IN MAJOR ETHICAL-DRUG MARKETS AND THE SHARE OF U.S. FIRMS IN FOREIGN MARKETS, 1975

Country	Sales Revenue ($ billions)	Share of the Global Market (percent)	Share of U.S. Firms in the Market (percent)
United States	6.9	17.2	n.a.
Japan	4.8	12.0	10
West Germany	3.4	8.5	15
France	2.8	7.0	15
Italy	2.0	5.0	10
Spain	1.2	3.0	25
United Kingdom	1.1	2.8	35
Rest of the world	17.8	44.5	n.a.
Total	40.0	100.0	

n.a. = not available.

SOURCE: The Bank of New York, *Investment Manager's Service, Progress Report,* December 16, 1976.

Appendix D
Beta and the Measurement of Risk in the Ethical Pharmaceutical Industry

Although all twelve firms in the sample that was used to estimate the cost of capital in the ethical pharmaceutical industry are classified in the Ethical Drug Industry (*Compustat* Code 2835), their operations include fields other than ethical drugs. The beta used to estimate the cost of capital of ethical-drug operations is that of the firm. Conceptually, however, the beta of a firm is a weighted average of the individual betas for each field of operation that the firm is involved in. Therefore, the beta of an ethical-drug firm may be a biased estimator for the beta of its ethical-drug operations if this differs from the beta of other operations of the firm.

Ethical-drug firms operate in a fairly wide range of fields in addition to ethical drugs. Three of these fields which assume a relatively important position are chemicals, cosmetics, and proprietary drugs. The average beta of firms classified in these industries is compared with the average beta value of ethical-drug firms as presented in table 34.

The figures in table 34 indicate that the risk in ethical-drug operations, as viewed by shareholders, is about equal to the risk in three other major fields in which ethical-drug firms operate. This observation appears to contradict the widespread belief that ethical-drug manufacture is a high-risk undertaking. The difference in conclusions may be rooted in the difference in the measures of risk that are used.

One measure of risk that has been used to demonstrate the high risk of ethical-drug operations is the high rate of attrition of ethical-drug R & D projects.[1] The total risk of ethical-drug operations, however, can be small even with a high attrition rate during the R & D process if each R & D project is small relative to the total R & D undertaking and if the failure rate in the market is relatively low.[2]

Another measure of risk is the variance of the annual accounting rate of return of firms over some time period. Fisher and Hall employ this measure of risk and conclude that some of the explanation for the high average rate of return of pharmaceutical firms is in their high risk.[3] The problems that make the accounting rate of return a biased estimator of the

TABLE 34
AVERAGE BETA OF FIRMS WITH OPERATIONS
TYPICAL TO ETHICAL-DRUG FIRMS

Industry	IND Code	No. of Firms	Average Beta Value
Drugs, ethical	2835	17	1.09
Chemical, major	2801	11	1.10
Cosmetics	2844	13	1.11
Drugs, proprietary	2836	10	1.12

SOURCE: The firms are those listed in the *Compustat* manual (Standard and Poor, *Compustat*, New York, 1975). Adjusted betas are from Merrill Lynch, *Security Risk Evaluation*, April 1977.

internal rate of return are discussed in chapter 2. If the measure of the rate of return is biased, it is likely that so will be any measure of risk derived from it. Indeed, Kenneth W. Clarkson found that correction of the accounting rate of return by capitalizing R & D and advertising expenditures reduces not only the accounting rate of return but also the variance of the rate of return.[4]

An alternative measure of risk is embodied in the beta of firms. Beta provides a measure of the risk of a firm as evaluated by its shareholders.[5] Unlike measures of risk that employ the variance of the returns, beta measures the covariance of the return of a security and the return on the market. It is quite possible that a security with a relatively high variance of return will have a relatively low covariance with the market, and thus will have relatively low risk.

Notes

1. H. A. Clymer, "The Changing Costs and Risks of Pharmaceutical Innovation," in *The Economics of Drug Innovation*, ed. J. D. Cooper (Washington, D.C.: The American University, 1970), pp. 109–24.

2. E. H. Mansfield, "Comment," in *The Economics of Drug Innovation*, ed. J. D. Cooper (Washington, D.C.: The American University, 1970), pp. 149–54.

3. I. N. Fisher and G. R. Hall, "Risk and Corporate Rate of Return," *Quarterly Journal of Economics*, vol. 82 (February 1969), pp. 79–92.

4. K. W. Clarkson, *Intangible Capital and Rates of Return* (Washington, D.C.: American Enterprise Institute, 1977).

5. See M. Blume, "On the Assessment of Risk," *Journal of Finance*, vol. 24 (March 1971), pp. 1–10.

Appendix E

Estimating Profit Margins, the Rate of Return, and the Cost of Capital for Ethical Pharmaceutical Drugs

The profit margin on sales is the fraction of sales revenue left after relevant expenditures have been subtracted, or:

$$M = \frac{\text{Sales revenue} - \text{Relevant expenditures}}{\text{Sales revenue}}$$

If the profit margin is known, we may estimate the net cash flow by multiplying sales revenue by the profit margin.

The internal rate of return on ethical drugs, r, can be estimated using the following equation

$$0 = (R_n + C_n)(1 + r)^n + \ldots + (R_o + C_o)(1 + r)^o \qquad \text{(E.1)}$$

$$+ \frac{MS_1}{1 + r} + \ldots + \frac{MS_m}{(1 + r)^m}$$

where $R_n \ldots R_o$ are research and development outlays in years n through o, $C_n \ldots C_o$ are other capital expenditures, $S_1 \ldots S_m$ are sales revenue in years 1 through m, and M is the profit margin on sales.

The internal rental cost of capital is defined as rC, where r is the internal rate of return on all projects and C is the amount of capital. The following proof shows that the traditional formula for the internal rate of return and the formula using the internal rental cost of capital are the same.

Assume that an investment project requires an initial cash outlay of A_o, and it yields a cash inflow of A_t, $t = 1, n$. Assume also that because of wear and tear a constant proportion λ of the original investment has to be replaced each year at a cost of λA_o. The internal rate of return for such a project is the value of r that satisfies

$$A_o = \sum_{t=1}^{n} \frac{A_t - \lambda A_o}{(1 + r)^t} + \frac{A_o}{(1 + r)^n}$$

ity $(1 + r)^n A_o = (1 + r)^n A_o$, we can derive

$$A_o = \sum_{t=1}^{n} \frac{rA_o}{(1 + r)^t} + \frac{A_o}{(1 + r)^n}$$

subtracting this amount from the preceding equation yields

$$0 = \sum_{t=1}^{n} \frac{A_t - \lambda A_o - rA_o}{(1 + r)^t}$$

In this last form, the initial cash outlay of A_o is replaced by the internal rental cost of capital rA_o.

Using the internal rental cost of capital concept, we can rewrite equation E.1 as

$$0 = R_n(1 + r)^n + \ldots + R_o(1 + r)^o + \frac{MS_1 - rDS_1}{1 + r} \qquad \text{(E.2)}$$

$$+ \ldots + \frac{MS_m - rDS_m}{(1 + r)^m}$$

where D is the ratio of capital to sales revenue $(D = C/S)$. The internal rate of return on ethical drugs will be estimated by using this equation.